The God of Joy *and the* Problem of Pain

The God of Joy *and the* Problem of Pain

BY JORGE ORDEIG CORSINI

Scepter

Published by Scepter Publishers, Inc.
info@scepterpublishers.org
www.scepterpublishers.org
800-322-8773
New York

Cover Art: *Portrait of the Boy Eutyches*, ca. AD 100–150. Encaustic on wood. Metropolitan Museum of Art, New York. www.metmuseum.org/art/collection/search/547951. Public Domain.
Cover Design: DeLight Design Studio
Page Design and Composition: Rose Design

Library of Congress Control Number: 2025943039
ISBN paperback: 978-0-93393-217-3
ISBN eBook: 978-0-93393-209-8

Printed in the United States of America

Contents

Introduction

Sooner or later, we all experience some type of suffering. All human beings have this in common. Who hasn't felt some type of pain? Who hasn't at some point asked, "Why is this happening to me?"

Nevertheless, no two people deal with pain in exactly the same way. We have all seen, personally or in the media, people who lead very comfortable lives but are unhappy, and others who, despite great pain, radiate joy and peace to everyone around them.

As far back as the emergence of philosophy, people have felt the need to consider the existence of joy and suffering. Despite great interest, we still have not managed to fully answer the questions arising from these conflicting realities.

The issue of suffering, in particular, carries a certain urgency for some Christians. By not understanding pain and failing to put it into proper focus, we may lose our joy and even begin to doubt God. This is the most severe consequence of an inability to respond positively to the problems posed by suffering.

My hope is that all readers may benefit from this book, regardless of academic background or personal experience. Pain and suffering are present in everyone's life, and we all need help to make sense of them. For this reason, I have avoided overly philosophical language and have limited the use of citations and footnotes.

For those who wish to delve deeper into the subject, I have included at the end some additional resources on the problem of pain. Much has been written, but I have included only those that I deem most relevant. Among them, I draw your attention to a book by Anglican author C. S. Lewis, *The Problem of Pain*, written from a more personal perspective than some, and a book by Carlos Cardona, *Metafísica del bien y del mal* (Metaphysics of Evil), authored from a more philosophical perspective.

In part one of this book, I aim to provide the most rational explanation possible for the causes of evil and pain in the world. While avoiding excessively philosophical language, I use a theoretical approach to explore the issue on an intellectual level.

In part two, I no longer address the problem as theoretical but rather explore what to do when we find ourselves in the middle of deep suffering. I offer advice on how to confront pain from a human perspective and then from a more supernatural, Christian viewpoint.

There are few dogmatic truths surrounding this subject. The majority of the ideas in this book are open to debate. There are only a handful of points that must be affirmed with the force of the Church's doctrine; I point them out. Regarding the rest, I caution that we are all entitled to our own perspectives—but it is important that we develop these viewpoints well.

At the end of the day, the problem remains unresolved: Joy and pain do coexist, and we do not know entirely why. I do not claim to have the final word on this, and it would be absurd to imply otherwise. But I do wish to help you, the reader, to reframe the question and find the best line of reasoning to personally make sense of pain. We are all seekers of truth, and any idea that may help us get closer is welcome.

PART I

Causes of Pain

I.

The Problem

The God of Joy

Before diving into the problem of suffering, I would like to make one initial observation. Almost all human experience is analogical, not digital. We live in a highly digitalized world, but it is worth remembering that most aspects of our lives cannot be reduced to zeros and ones, to yes or no, but actually should be understood in terms of more or less, better or worse. The goal is not to just be a student but to be a good student; not just to enroll in a course but to really study. We can be better or worse students, all the while being students.

The same is true of anything we set out to be, whether drivers, athletes, civil servants, cooks, or parents. Whatever our jobs or endeavors may be, the important thing is to seek improvement and, if possible, reach a certain degree of excellence.

This also applies to Christianity. The goal is not just to wear the title "Christian," but to be good Christians. Simply having the title is not enough. We may enroll in a course but not benefit from it at all. If we do not attend the class, never crack open a book, and fail to show up for the tests, then what have we gained by being "students"? Nothing. We might as well not be students at all. Likewise for Christianity: We may be on the official roster of Christians, but all the while be living like pagans. If so, are we answering our call to be disciples of Christ?

How can we measure our Christianity? How can we know if we are good Christians? Academic students are often given tests, which can prove a concrete measure of demonstrated knowledge. Do Christians have any kind of measure to determine whether we are doing a good job?

I believe we have several standards. Undoubtedly, one measure is our concern for others, our charity. But there is another very clear indicator: the way in which we understand God. We can approach God as a loving Father who goes out of his way for our happiness and joy, or we can see him as a terrible and puzzling being, unconcerned with our desire for happiness and even the cause of our problems.

Christians say again and again that God is the God of love and of joy. This is a core teaching of Christianity, according to the Gospels. In 2013, Pope Francis authored a document of guidance titled *Evangelii gaudium* (The Joy of the Gospel). Christianity has always affirmed this truth, and the Pontiff gave it an even stronger emphasis.[1]

---

1. Francis, Apostolic Exhortation on the Proclamation of the Gospel in Today's World *Evangelii gaudium* (November 24, 2013), nos. 4–5. www.vatican.va.

To be a Christian is, at its core, to trust in God. If we did not trust God, we would have a hard time claiming to be Christian. But we can only truly trust in someone whom we love and by whom we feel loved. We cannot trust an enemy, or someone who hurts us or causes us to suffer.

If we somehow get it in our heads that God is responsible for our suffering, how difficult it will be for us to trust him! Therefore, the problem of pain hits close to the essence of Christianity. In other words, if we mistakenly attribute the problem of evil to God, we may distrust him, distance ourselves from him, and have our faith shaken.

Only if we see God as the God of joy, love, and peace can we trust him and truly be Christians.

The Scandal of Evil

In stark contrast with the God of joy, we have what is often called the "scandal of evil." The *Catechism of the Catholic Church* explains it as follows: "If God the Father almighty, the Creator of the ordered and good world, cares for all his creatures, why does evil exist?"[2]

A scandal, in theological terms, is any action, word, or image that might cause a person to sin, or to turn away from God. In this sense, pain and suffering,

---

2. *Catechism of the Catholic Church*, 2nd ed. (Libreria Editrice Vaticana—United States Conference of Catholic Bishops, 2000), no. 309.

when not understood correctly, are real causes of scandal. They separate us from God.

The blame for the scandal, logically, does not fall on God. Neither is the suffering itself to blame, but rather our own reactions when faced with pain or evil. This is why we can attest to the fact that pain is a touchstone of the Christian faith. It is a test of whether deep down we are truly Christians or have only subscribed to a superficial religion, simply "enrolled" as Christians.

It is evident that an atheist does not face this problem. If the world were a random result of chaos, the exception would be something working correctly. In a world without God, the norm would be chaos, collision, and intrinsic disorder, with the logical side effects of harm and suffering. For an atheist, pain and evil can be the source of other problems, but doubting the goodness of God is not one of them.

There is also no problem for someone who subscribes to a dualistic belief system. If there is one good deity and another evil, then both good and evil have a justifiable explanation. Neither is there great difficulty if we consider God as the "great architect of the universe," as such a god would have set the universe spinning and then disengaged for all of history.

But if we believe in a loving and caring God, how can we explain the existence of evil? How can we reconcile evil with the love of God? This is the unavoidable issue, the question that has been asked as far back as ancient Greece. People of faith cannot be confronted with this problem and shrug our shoulders.

Christianity has always been able to confidently balance faith and reason. God is the ultimate source of all truth, and an effort to understand diverse realities of this world will always lead us to a better understanding of God, within our human limitations.

For this reason, this book is written for people who have at least a small amount of faith in a loving God, those who may find most perplexing the possible contradiction between the God of joy and the reality of pain and suffering.

Perhaps now that we find ourselves in the twenty-first century, we may have the tools to give a more comprehensive response to this question than in past centuries. In any case, the problem is complicated and does not have an easy or exact solution. We must be willing to take our time and think it through carefully.

The Real Existence of Evil

Evil exists. This is an indisputable fact for most people. Even so, it is in our best interest to start off by recognizing this reality.[3] At certain times evil presents itself as the mere absence of good: for example, when a person is born blind or crippled. At other times, evil appears in the form of conscious and voluntary

3. It is true that, within a rigorous metaphysical worldview, evil does not have an ontological existence of its own, but rather is the absence of good. See St. Thomas Aquinas, *Summa Theologica* 1.48. Even so, in this same article Aquinas recognizes that evil is found within things (1.48.2). In this sense we can affirm the existence of evil showing up frequently in our lives.

harm. Sometimes it is a natural disaster, and at other times, it is simply an uneasiness with the world around us or with our own identity. Whatever form it may take, evil is anything that produces pain and suffering in us.

Some people deny the objectivity of good and evil and believe that what is good for some people may be considered bad by others. However, for our purposes, we can leave aside this type of philosophical relativism. Evil is that which causes harm to us as humans, as persons, as members of society. At times, we feel its effects physically, and other times internally. At times, something causes us real harm, and we realize it only after some time has passed. But even when an evil initially goes unnoticed, it is evil nonetheless, something that has done damage.

We could briefly define good as that which perfects us as persons, that which helps in our development and enables us to become whole as human beings. Evil, on the other hand, is that which harms us, that which hinders us from reaching the fullness we all seek.

Evil, by its definition, harms us. This harm is evident when we feel pain, whether it be physical or mental. When a microbe causes harm in my body, I feel the pain. If I am hit by something, the same. And when someone treats me poorly, I also feel a pain on the inside that lets me know an injustice has been committed. Our reaction to the harm caused by evil is always pain.

Pain, in turn, has a specific effect on humankind: suffering. While pain is a natural reaction to harm, whether it be physical or social, suffering is a secondary reaction. We suffer because we are conscious of the pain and many times, because we realize the purposelessness of the pain. This is suffering: the internal reflection of pain, and a sense of desperation—be it great or small—when faced with pain that often seems to make no sense.

There are then four steps: evil, harm, pain, and suffering. From a psychological point of view, the real problem is suffering. The issue that we normally refer to as the problem of pain is not so much the pain itself, but rather the suffering that ensues. Suffering can hit us with an overwhelming force, lead to a state of nearly acute depression, and cause us to wonder about the purpose of our distress.

Suffering is a companion that appears many times throughout our lives. John Paul II said, "In whatever form, suffering seems to be, and is, almost *inseparable from man's earthly existence.*"[4] But suffering is always a consequence of pain, which in turn has as its root some type of evil. In most cases, suffering is caused by real pain, be it physical or internal. At other times, the evil is imagined, as is the case with some pathological depressions, but the resulting pain and suffering are no less real.

---

4. John Paul II, Apostolic Letter on the Christian Meaning of Human Suffering *Salvifici doloris* (February 11, 1984), no. 3. www.vatican.va.

Because they are intrinsically connected, in this work we will refer to the four steps almost interchangeably. At times we will focus more on the root evil and at times on the resulting pain and suffering, depending on the line of reasoning. After all, they are practically inseparable.

Is God to Blame?

No sooner do we find ourselves deep in a well of suffering than we cannot help but wonder why and almost automatically ask, "Why is this happening to me?"

Later we will see that this is a trick question; it has no possible answer. Nevertheless, it is a question that inevitably leads to angst-filled and depressing neurosis. Since human beings cannot live with such an important question left unanswered, the instinct is to search for some kind of answer. The first answer that comes to mind for some people is "Because God wanted this to happen."

This assertion, logically, provides an answer to the troublesome question. We have a response, although a poor one. If this is the only solution we can find, all our suffering channels into resentment toward this God who has been (mysteriously) capable of harming us or allowing others to do so.

Those who do not have deep Christian roots may easily fall into this line of thinking. They have heard that God knows everything and can do anything. Logically, they do not understand how it is possible for this God to stand by and do nothing to take away the pain they are feeling. They start to think of God as a being who takes pleasure in human suffering, or at the very least, who is indifferent. As a result, they foster a feeling of distrust and resentment toward this God, who is responsible for all that is wrong in the world.

This problem can be aggravated by certain priests who preach with excessively providential and naive overtones. It is not uncommon to hear in some churches, especially at funerals, explanations that in one way or another blame God for the death of a loved one.

I once met a mother who had not set foot inside a church for ten years. The reason was that she had lost her six-year-old son. The priest who gave the homily at his funeral had, with the best intentions, said more or less the following: "Your son was so sweet that God wanted to take him to be with himself." If this phrase is taken literally, it seems to imply that God had caused the death of the boy. The mother, who believed just that, jumped to the following conclusion: "I do not want to have anything more to do with a God who snatches away my children!" This is a logical and reasonable reaction. Nevertheless, the premise is faulty. God never, for any reason, kills anyone.

We would do well to remember that, when we encounter deep suffering, we can easily become desperate. When this happens, the mind is no longer in control, and our emotions take the reins. When we are not thinking logically and are swayed by the less-than-rational impulses of our feelings, we can start to think and believe any type of nonsense.

If for some reason we begin to blame God for the bad things that happen, we will undoubtedly arrive at one conclusion: God is dangerous and the source of evil in the world. We would then develop such a deformed, ridiculous idea of God that we would walk away from him. Most religions, especially Christianity, urge us to trust God, but it would be impossible to trust in a being we view as the cause of our pain. Instead of trust, we might develop hate and try to get as far away from him as possible.

Doing so would inevitably take us to a place of despair and sadness. If we have even a small amount of faith to believe in a Creator and omnipotent God, but view this God as a threat to humankind, then there is no possible solution. Our lives are doomed to the horror of suffering beyond repair.

Persons with a stronger faith—perhaps without having thought it through so much—might say, "But by suffering here on earth, we have heaven to gain." While this is true in some sense, many people would think, "I prefer to be happy on earth, and we'll see what happens next." It would not be hard to find ourselves almost agreeing more with the second opinion than the first. The first idea (suffer here with the hope of heaven later) is what led Karl Marx to believe that religion was alienating for humanity. Effectively, if we are dealing with a religion like this, Marx's logic is understandable, in as much as it is based on a mistaken premise.

To highlight this truth, I bring your attention to a statement from Pope Francis. In his letter *The Joy of the Gospel*, the Pontiff writes,

> It is no longer possible to claim that religion should be restricted to the private sphere and that it exists only to prepare souls for heaven. We know that God wants his children to be happy in this world too.[5]

This is quite significant: God wants us to be happy, here, on earth. This is the will of God. Additionally, he is preparing flawless happiness for us in heaven.

The intention is not to minimize the importance of heaven. Any person of faith clearly knows that the future life is infinitely more important than life here on earth. But God does not want us to gain heaven at the cost of suffering. God expects us to reach heaven because of our generosity and love. And this is the way to happiness here on earth. God wants us to be happy, both on earth and in heaven.

The Complexity of the Problem

As we have seen, the problem of pain turns out to be arduous and complex. Humanity has been dealing with it for centuries, and we still have yet to find a reasonable explanation. This tells us that we are facing a real difficulty. If the problem had a simple solution,

5. Francis, *Evangelii gaudium*, no. 182.

that would have been discovered long ago. Therefore, if anyone claims to have a simple answer to the problem of pain, it is likely to be a false solution, or at the very least incomplete.

Why is this problem so complex? There are several reasons.

Prior to the current age, people had little insight into nature. This led great writers to discuss the problem of evil and pain with less information than we have available to us today. Especially with regard to physical evil, the scope was lacking, and the conclusions proved unhelpful from a modern point of view. Currently, we are more equipped than ever to better understand some of the "whys" surrounding pain.

Nevertheless, when we set out to reflect on pain, we automatically encounter two significant issues: human free will and the omnipotence of God. These are not simple issues; and if we err in understanding either one, suffering becomes almost incomprehensible.

The problem becomes even more urgent when evil affects us personally. In part one, we have set out to find the most rational explanation possible of the problem of pain and evil in general terms. But such an understanding is vastly different from the one that emerges when we are personally affected by intense pain. It is one thing to understand the problem of pain theoretically, and another thing altogether to accept pain when it shows up on our doorstep. In part two, we set out to expound on some ideas that will help us to face pain in a more pragmatic way.

The most eloquent example of this dichotomy was given to us by C. S. Lewis. His book, *The Problem of Pain*, is one of the best that has been written on this subject. Despite this, when his wife died, Lewis wrote another book entitled *A Grief Observed*, in which he describes his internal agony when faced with the inexplicable pain of losing his wife. When suffering touched him personally, he lost sight of what he had written in his previous book. In the midst of his consternation, Lewis writes that God is "the great cosmic sadist." He then, in subsequent pages, begins to rectify his thinking as he accepts the pain of the absence of his wife—but he leaves us a moving testimony of the contrast between understanding the problem theoretically and the near desperation experienced when affected personally.

Adding to the complexity, as we will see in the following chapter, some ways of speaking (and preaching) have only served to complicate the issue. It seems evident that we are not only susceptible to faulty "understanding" but also, on certain occasions, to faulty "explanations."

In spite of all the difficulties, having some understanding of the problem of pain—even if it be partial or incomplete—can help us to confront pain when it finds us. By contrast, a mistaken understanding can lead us to feel desperate and miserable.

II.

Initial Thoughts

Moral Evil and Natural Evil

When we face a complex problem, it is helpful, whenever possible, to deal with each of its facets one by one.

The first and most obvious necessary distinction is to recognize two large categories of evil present in the world. We are going to call *moral evil* any wrong that in one way or another depends on the free will of humans. And we will call *natural evil* anything that is a product of nature, independent of the voluntary intervention of any person.

It is a classic distinction, but we do well to be reminded of it. Therefore, we will address these two types of evil in two separate chapters. Although sometimes the two may appear intertwined, the distinction is justified, at least for the purpose of studying them.

Pious Talk and Real Talk

The second necessary distinction is more complicated. In fact, it is one of the most common causes for confusion when dealing with this issue.

Even when using the same language, we may have very different ways of speaking. For example, the language of poets is different from the language on the street. In the same way, lawyers, scientists, and sailors all have their own languages. They may use the same words, but with very different meanings.

A poet may write that the protagonist has cherry lips and cheeks like peaches, but no one believes that this is real; we all know it should not be taken literally.

These variations in language create a subproblem when people attempt to explain pain. For centuries, priests have used a pious language to speak about death and pain. This language is valid if the listener holds the key to interpret it: if the listener is also a pious person with a strong love for God and a desire for the will of God.

Let's look at a few examples. Previously, we mentioned a priest who, at the funeral of a child said, "He was so sweet that God wanted to take him away." The priest was not stupid, nor did he intend to accuse God of having killed a child. His goal was to help the suffering mother come to terms with the death of her son and to comfort her with the pious idea that the boy was now happy with God in heaven. But as this mother was unable to correctly interpret the priest's pious language, she misinterpreted the comment and ended up believing what she had clearly heard: God had taken away her son.

In the same way, many people of faith, when confronted with a tough season of sickness or family hurt, make comments such as, "Let's see when God will stop sending me so many trials." These people are convinced, or at least their words imply, that the sickness and problems they are experiencing have come from God. This may be because, when the sickness appeared, some pious person said something like, "This sickness is a gift of God. It will help you draw closer to him and teach you the virtue of patience." When a person is faced with an incurable disease, for example, there is almost always someone who asserts "We must accept the will of God."

These statements may comfort a person with faith and love for God, as they serve to remind us that God is always close to those who suffer, and that with suffering comes the promise of eternal life with God. For a person who has prayed the Lord's Prayer many times in faith, it may be comforting to think that by accepting the sickness or death of a loved one, we are putting into practice "thy will be done." Furthermore, it is true that, when dealing with pain, we become aware of a will of God that we should love; we will discuss this in the last chapter.

That said, these phrases cannot be interpreted literally as if heard in passing on the street and given their most typical meanings. If someone with little Christian background, a weak faith, or scant love for God hears something like this, the person may conclude that God is the one who sends sickness and death in order to test us or for reasons we don't know. And this would be a grave error.

Understanding this point is necessary for addressing the problem of pain. Poetic language is different from pious language and theological, scientific, or legal language, and they are all different from the casual language we use on the street. Many saints throughout the centuries have bravely accepted pain and death as coming from the hand of God, but this is pious language and does not leave room for literal interpretation. If such pious talk were understood literally, the problem of pain would lead to no other conclusion than to blame God for every bad thing that happens to us.

For centuries, people with strong Christian roots—particularly in European countries—have had a wide enough knowledge base to understand this pious talk. But today, many westerners do not have the religious culture needed for understanding this language and they hear something very different. Confusion is the inevitable result.

Pope Francis, in his letter *Evangelii gaudium*, warns us about this problem:

> There are times when the faithful, in listening to completely orthodox language, take away something alien to the authentic Gospel of Jesus Christ, because that language is alien to their own way of speaking to and understanding one another. With the holy intent of communicating the truth about God and humanity, we sometimes give them a false god or a human ideal which is not really Christian.[1]

1. Francis, *Evangelii gaudium*, no. 41.

He is pointing to the exact same problem we are dealing with here: pious talk versus cultural communication. If we are unable to translate, unable to speak to each person in his or her own language, we risk giving people a false god, as the Pope says.

One further example which is especially clear and relevant to the issue we are dealing with: Quite frequently, in educational Christian homilies or talks you might hear the expression "love the cross." To the person with spiritual formation this has a clear meaning, but the literal meaning is absurd. If the tone is pious or Christian, the statement has two possible meanings: "love Christ on the cross," or "carry your burden peacefully and patiently for love of Christ crucified." We can even translate it with a more mystical meaning as "seek sacrifice to be spiritually united with Christ." Any of these possible meanings would be clear to a pious person.

But if understood plainly, "love the cross" would mean one of the following two options: either to love a piece of wood (which would be completely silly) or to love a symbol of torture, a clear indication that we urgently need psychiatric help, since masochism is a pathological deviation from any sensible way of thinking. We cannot confuse the two languages; neither can we use pious talk with a person who lacks the ability to understand it.

In this book I have made every effort to use only the most direct language possible. Only in part two might you find slightly more pious language in a few places. The consideration of evil and pain allows for pious language in a few rare exceptions.

God, Creator of All Good

If we hope to reach any kind of conclusion about the problem of pain, we must affirm the truth that God is the creator of all good in the universe—not of evil.

In the Mass, at the end of the Church's oldest Eucharistic Prayer, the Roman Canon (*Canon Romano*), we say the following:

> Christ our Lord[,]
> [t]hrough whom
> you continue to make all these good things, O Lord;
> you sanctify them, fill them with life,
> bless them, and bestow them upon us.[2]

In this the Church believes: God, Christ, is the creator and bestower of all good things, not of the bad. Any opposing belief would be contrary to the Christian faith.

To confirm this, we need not look any further than the first chapters of the Book of Genesis. Even though the language is symbolic (another type of language that we must know how to interpret), these chapters make very clear that God created humankind to be happy. In verse 28 of the first chapter, we read that God said to the man, "Be fruitful and multiply, and fill the earth and subdue it; and have dominion over the fish of the sea and over the birds of the air and over

2. *Roman Missal, Third Typical Edition* (United States Conference of Catholic Bishops, 2011), nos. 30–31.

every living thing that moves upon the earth." Or in a more modern and colloquial language, "Live and grow and be happy." This is what God expects of us. This is what God has given to humans: an entire universe in which to live and grow. And a few verses later, we read the conclusion that "God saw everything that he had made, and behold, it was very good" (Gn 1:31).

God has given us a wonderful world to live in, a life to enjoy. He created us to know how to love and to bring us to heaven. These realities are all good, all gifts from God.

And yet, we sometimes distrust God and may even view him as a danger. Pope John Paul II, in the encyclical *Dominum et vivificantem*, speaking of original sin and the resulting separation from God, affirms:

> Here we find ourselves at the very center of what could be called the "anti-Word," that is to say the "anti-truth." For the truth about man becomes falsified: who man is and what are the impassable limits of his being and freedom. This "anti-truth" is possible because at the same time there is a complete falsification of the truth about who God is. God the Creator is placed in a state of suspicion, indeed of accusation, in the mind of the creature. For the first time in human history there appears the perverse "genius of suspicion." He seeks to "falsify" Good itself; the absolute Good, which precisely in the work of creation has manifested itself as the Good which gives in an

> inexpressible way: as *bonum diffusivum sui*, as creative love. . . .
>
> For in spite of all the witness of creation and of the salvific economy inherent in it, the spirit of darkness is capable of showing God as an enemy of his own creature, and in the first place as an enemy of man, as a source of danger and threat to man. In this way Satan manages to sow in man's soul the seed of opposition. . . . Man is challenged to become the adversary of God![3]

The sad reality is that we so easily become suspicious of God. We have trouble recognizing him as the giver of good and often end up distrusting him, believing that, in some way, he is responsible for our troubles. If we can understand the problem of pain correctly, we will be able to abandon this suspicious view of God and to trust him and thank him for the many good things he has given us.

---

3. John Paul II, Encyclical on the Holy Spirit in the Life of the Church and the World *Dominum et vivificantem (*May 18, 1986), nos. 37 and 38.

III.

God and Moral Evil

Moral Evil

As we carefully reflect on suffering and pain, we must remember that most suffering in the world is a product of human action: war, injustice, murder, fraud, theft, infidelity, loneliness, contempt, falsehood . . . and a long etcetera that we can attribute to none other than the free and voluntary behavior of humans.

Nature also supplies us with its own evils—diseases, natural disasters, and death—but the list is much shorter, and these evils often produce less suffering. Most difficult to comprehend, and with no logical explanation, are the evils that we inflict on one another. These evils are by no means necessary, yet they cause us to suffer to the point of desperation.

And no less serious is the harm that we bring upon ourselves. Each one of us is responsible for our own life, and misguided priorities can have disastrous consequences over time. It is sufficient to consider the many lives that have been destroyed by alcohol or by drugs, yet no one is forced into substance abuse. But the list of self-inflicted evils does not end with addictions. In many cases a person must take personal responsibility for a broken marriage, an affair, the mismanagement of a company, poor health choices, or simply a failure to gain an education. We can all say at some point, "I am the person who makes myself suffer!"

Ultimately a large part of the pain we experience is caused by problems of our own making. This sums up what is often referred to as the "mystery of evil." Why do humans, capable of doing good, choose to do evil, knowing it is wrong?

It is true that many times we do bad things simply by mistake, either not realizing it or failing to make careful decisions. It is important to remember that carelessness is a sin; many of our mistakes are purely due to failing to think before we act. But we cannot deny that at times we do wrong and are *completely aware* of our actions, clearly knowing that we are causing harm to others or to ourselves.

A complete explanation for this enigma is beyond the limits of this book. For now, it is sufficient to say that a large part of the evil suffered here on earth is directly caused by human behavior. In theological terms, we can conclude that moral suffering is a product of sin. Furthermore, sin is identified with moral evil.[1] There is nothing recognized by the Church as a sin that is not also an evil, something harmful to humankind.

---

1. It may be helpful to note that the notion of "sin," in comparison to the notion of "moral evil," carries an additional component of willingness. Sin is to *voluntarily* do wrong, in contrast to other evils that we may personally commit, but without sufficient knowledge.

Let's take marriage problems as an example. When we take a deeper look, we discover there is always some behavior that Christian doctrine would consider sin, such as pride, arrogance, selfishness, infidelity, or laziness. Some of these sins are well-known "bad ideas," and others may simply be motivated by a lack of responsibility or a misunderstanding.

The Power of Freedom

The mystery of evil in the human heart goes hand in hand with another big anthropological question: human freedom. All moral evil is directly related to the misuse of our freedom.

The main problem stems from the fact that freedom is inextricably linked to responsibility. We often underestimate the tremendous power of freedom in the life of each individual and in the development of society. To excuse our wrong actions, we sometimes attempt to deny that we have acted freely. If this were the case, we would be absolved of our responsibility. It is therefore necessary for us to take a closer look at some aspects of our freedom and its impact on our lives.

In general, the question of freedom is as complex as the problem of evil. The two are closely linked, and our understanding of freedom has clear implications on the explanation for evil. Without delving into a study of freedom itself, we can define it as the ability to decide to lead our life as we wish, taking into account the limitations imposed by the freedom of those around us and the inherent limitations of human nature.

We use our freedom to build our lives, based on the opportunities and choices that freedom offers. The ways we use our freedom influence the lives of others. In turn, the ways others use their freedom influence our lives. Each of our actions has consequences, which impact us and can also impact others, for society is comprised of our interconnected lives. This interconnectedness often leads to good but can also lead to evil—with the result that we cause one another to suffer, whether we act with bad intentions or we act out of ignorance.[2]

It is true that many influences determine the course of our lives, but while they may restrict our freedom, they do not negate it. In any case, it would be unacceptable to place the blame on God. We are not God's puppets. We do what we wish, or what we can, or what others let us do, but we do not act under any overriding decision of God's that would negate our personal freedom. We construct our own lives. We may choose to build them on the commands and advice of God or, if we so desire, go completely outside of the bounds he has set in place.

The power of our freedom is a profound mystery. To put it simply, in this life, if God wants one thing

---

2. Sin, in fact, has detrimental effects not only on the one who commits the sin but on the whole Church, as each sin disrupts the unity of the Body of Christ. "It wounds the nature of man and injures human solidarity" (*Catechism of the Catholic Church*, no. 1849).

and we do the opposite, our will is done, not God's. This means that, regarding concrete actions here on earth, as amazing as it may seem, man's will prevails over God's.

Of course, upon closer inspection, it is God who willed it to work like this. So then, when we go against the expressed will of God, we continue to fulfill God's will that we be free. Nevertheless, when faced with any given decision, God may want one thing, for which he has given us a clear commandment, and we are free to act in opposition.

St. Thomas Aquinas[3] explains this by making a distinction between universal providence (God's will) and particular providence. A person, acting freely, is fulfilling the *universal* will of God, which is that we be free. But this same freedom allows for a person to go against the *particular* will of God, to commit murder or embezzlement, for example.

Without a doubt, it is comforting to know that whatever we do, God will in the end renew the entire universe and make the *new heaven* and the *new earth* described by St. John in the Book of Revelation. But this does not minimize our responsibility in using our personal freedom with which, in any given situation, we may act contrary to the will of God and cause great harm to others and ourselves.

In the world there are many sins; this is certain. And every sin is a circumstance in which God has

---

3. Aquinas, *Summa Theologica* 1.103.

desired one thing and we the opposite; what has been done was not what God desired. A traditional definition of sin is precisely *to act contrary to the will of God.*

It is to our advantage to use excessively religious language sparingly. We have all heard the phrase "God willing." This refrain is often repeated in a pious tone of acceptance. It will prove a comfort for some, but not for all. In this life, especially in concrete day-to-day happenings, what takes place is what we wanted, not always what "God willed."[4]

Each time a person commits an atrocity, he or she is behaving in opposition to the commandments and the will of God. God does not stop us; he respects our freedom. He lets us do whatever we feel like, even if it is something terrible. If people want to set off bombs, for example, God will not stop them, despite these actions being in no way what God would want.

Even the crucifixion of Jesus was an example of human free will. God the Father did not send his Son into the world "to be killed"; he sent him to save the world from sin. It was we who refused to listen

---

4. A clarification is needed to avoid the risk of falling into Pelagianism, a heresy that denies the concept of original sin and claims that human beings can take their own steps toward doing good without the help of divine grace. In these lines we have made no reference to the grace of God in the soul. Part of the Church's doctrine is the necessity of grace for doing good works. A decision to do good is preceded and accompanied by the grace of God in the soul. Likewise, a decision to do wrong is our will—which has been damaged by the effects of sin—opposing the suggestions of grace. But in any case, God's grace never annuls our freedom.

and who condemned him to death, at great pain to the Father.

Ultimately, we must recognize and affirm the power of freedom with all its consequences. Calvinists have traditionally denied personal freedom for the doctrine of predestination, believing humans to have no freedom under the absolute sovereignty God has over salvation and damnation, a doctrine that paints God as a senseless controller.

So then, does God ever intervene in human history? We will take a look at Divine Providence in chapter six. For now, inasmuch as it relates to human freedom, we must affirm that yes, God does have a hand in history through those who freely choose to do his will in their lives.[5] As a matter of fact, these are the saints: people who, through their own actions, have contributed to accomplishing the will of God here on earth. This is another important reason for the necessity that we all become saints. It is only when we freely seek to do what God desires that we begin to take part in building a society in line with God's loving design.

But even when we do what we understand to be the will of God, we are each no less personally responsible for our actions. We cannot transfer our responsibility to God, and the Bible affirms this. It was written

---

5. Pope Benedict XVI explains the following: "Nor has the Lord been absent from subsequent Church history: he encounters us ever anew, *in the men and women* who reflect his presence." Benedict XVI, Encyclical Letter on Christian Love *Deus caritas est* (December 25, 2005), no. 17. www.vatican.va. Emphasis added.

long ago in the Book of Sirach: "Before a man are life and death, and whichever he chooses will be given to him" (15:17). Our choices have not been determined for us by God. What we choose is what we will get.

The Limits of Divine Omnipotence

If we can agree that the responsibility for moral evil lies with humanity, and not with God, this question follows: Why doesn't God keep it from happening? Is he not omnipotent? Why won't he prevent us from doing evil?

Here we find ourselves faced with another important but often misunderstood truth: divine omnipotence. Lewis's book *The Problem of Pain* has a crucial chapter dedicated to the omnipotence of God. Effectively, if this characteristic is not understood, there is then no way to understand the questions left open by suffering.

A person on the street hears that God is all powerful and thinks, "So then God can do whatever he feels like." This is a normal understanding of "omnipotence": absolute impulsivity. For this reason, when I have been asked in other contexts, "Isn't God omnipotent?" I have always answered, "No, God is not omnipotent. At least, not in the way you are thinking."

Let me explain a little further. At certain times, I have proposed the following to a group of well-informed Christians: "Think about the planets revolving around their orbits. Could God suddenly cause them to orbit in the opposite direction?"

Most people answer yes, God can do whatever he pleases. Some have nuanced the answer by saying that God could do it but would not want to.

That is not true. It is easy to forget that God is not only omnipotent, but also deeply coherent. If we, with our human nature, had the power of God, the planets would not continue a single day uninterrupted in their orbits. We would have them moving left, moving right, skipping all around. But this is not God. Once he has set his will, he *cannot* change; he does not contradict himself.

And the distinction between what God can do and wants to do is not valid. His capabilities and his will align.[6]

Therefore, although it may seem strange to some people, the power of God has its limits. It is not an arbitrary omnipotence. According to Catholic theology, God is omnipotent in every way that does not imply a contradiction.[7] He cannot will or carry out anything contradictory in and of itself. He cannot desire or create a square that is round, nor red that is blue, nor a good that is evil. The same is true of his promises. When he has promised one thing, he cannot go back. He cannot contradict himself. God is the limit of his own omnipotence.

---

6. The connection between God's ability and will is an essential topic that requires a serious theological analysis. See, for example, St. Thomas Aquinas, *Summa Theologica* 1.25.5.1.

7. Aquinas, *Summa Theologica* 1.25.3. In general, the six articles of question 25 sufficiently clarify the limits of divine omnipotence.

This is key for understanding evil. God has created us as free beings and he will not take away our freedom. If a man takes a machine gun and goes into a school to kill children (as has happened in the United States), God will not prevent him. God made him to be free and he will not take away that freedom, no matter how wrongly used.

Or as Lewis says,

> You may attribute miracles to Him, but not nonsense. This is no limit to His power. . . . It remains true that all *things* are possible with God: the intrinsic impossibilities are not things but nonentities.[8]

For people to be simultaneously free and not free is an intrinsic impossibility, or nonsense.

Why Freedom?

If all moral evils stem from the free actions of humans, why was it God's desire that we be free? With a lengthy list of wars, genocides, murders, torture, and other means humans have invented to harm one another, the question does not seem to be insignificant.

The answer is that humans, without freedom, would cease to be human. We would be another animal, perhaps something more intelligent, but without the most essential human attribute: the capacity for love.

---

8. C. S. Lewis, "Divine Omnipotence," in *The Problem of Pain* (Centenary Press, 1940).

To be capable of love inevitably demands freedom. To love, we must be able to choose whom to love. A forced love is not love. When God created people, he was looking for someone with whom he could share love, a creature whom God could love for his own sake, and who could reciprocate this love freely because he wanted to.

This is the great reason for our freedom. If it were not for our freedom, we would experience less suffering, but we would be incapable of experiencing deeper happiness, which is always a result of love.

In the Parable of the Prodigal and His Brother, Jesus tells the story of a father who had two sons, one of whom requested his inheritance so that he could go off and spend it living recklessly. And the father gave it to him! He could have said no, but he did not (Lk 15:11–32). It would have been easy for God to create slaves without freedom, but this is not what he desired. His hope is that we learn to freely choose to love and obey him. He does not want slave-like submission, but childlike love.

It would be nonsense to accuse God of having given us freedom if freedom were an evil.

IV.

Does God "Permit" Evil?

The Term "Permit"

Most theologians—including St. Thomas Aquinas and St. Augustine, two of the most notable in history—used the term *permit* when referencing the problem of evil. Likewise, the *Catechism of the Catholic Church* uses the term in paragraph 311:

> God is in no way, directly or indirectly, the cause of moral evil. He permits it, however, because he respects the freedom of his creatures and, mysteriously, knows how to derive good from it.

And continuing in this same point, St. Augustine is cited:

> For almighty God . . . , because he is supremely good, would never allow any evil whatsoever to exist in his works if he were not so all-powerful and good as to cause good to emerge from evil itself.[1]

Therefore, both leading theologians and the Magisterium of the Catholic Church affirm that God

1. Augustine of Hippo, *Enchiridion de fide, spe et caritate*, 3.11.

permits evil. Nevertheless, part of the confusion of so many Christians when faced with the problem of pain and evil has its roots in the incorrect use of the term *permit*. We will try to explain further.

As we have said, in the same language there are diverse sublanguages, among others theological language, which diverges significantly from colloquial language. St. Thomas, or the *Catechism*, before using the term *permit*, have made quite clear that God is not the cause of any evil, especially moral evil. However, a person on the street may hear a priest say that God permits evil and apply connotations that the word carries in its everyday use.

Ordinarily, when a person permits harm, that person is in some way responsible for that harm. For example, if the manager of a bank branch permits the teller to embezzle funds, both the teller and the manager would—if caught—end up in jail. The manager is guilty (as an accomplice or coconspirator) of the teller's theft. I am unaware if in other languages there is an equivalent to the term *permit* that does not imply guilt, but in this language, the word normally carries a connotation of responsibility.

This particular meaning of *permit* must never be applied to God. If by affirming that God permits evil we are in some way claiming that he is responsible for it, we are committing a serious error, which is also condemned by the Church. In the same paragraph of the *Catechism*, we read: "God is in no way, directly or indirectly, the cause of moral evil."

We said at the beginning that there are few dogmas on the problem of evil. But this is one of them: God does not contribute in any way to moral evil. Therefore, if we wish to use the term *permit,* this usage should not in the slightest imply that we are accusing God of causing evil, not even by omission.

However, if in popular usage the term inextricably carries the concept of joint responsibility, it may be more accurate to say that God never permits moral evil.

God Forbids Evil

If we are driving and we come to an intersection, there are two possibilities: either a lefthand turn is permitted or it is forbidden. It will never be both permitted and forbidden.

So then, how can we say that God "permits" murder, theft, or unjust war? A person with the best intentions may ask in exasperation, "How is it possible that God permits war?" This is logical, as we have heard it said many times that God permits evil, and so we believe it, applying the connotations of guilt that are implied in the colloquial use of *permit.*

It is necessary to say loudly and repeatedly that not only does God not permit any moral evil, but rather that he strictly forbids it. We are forbidden to murder, to steal, to lie, to be unfaithful in marriage. These are not just forbidden; they are not permitted! How can we say that God "permits" the murder of a child? God forbids it resoundingly.

But as we have said, we humans do as we please. When we come to an intersection and find a clear sign forbidding lefthand turns, we may run the red light and turn left if we please.

But in so doing, we are not doing something that is permitted. On the contrary, we are doing something forbidden.

When a theologian affirms that God permits evil, he is saying that God does not prevent the free action of humans. God does not occupy himself with constant "miracles" to avoid instances of people doing wrong. Count on evil as an inevitable consequence of freedom, as we have explained in the previous chapter. All the same, we are reminded that the providence of God will finally bring all things to God at the end of time. In conclusion, God will have the last word in the Last Judgment.[2]

When priests and theologians use the term *permit*, they are affirming a completely orthodox doctrine that is misunderstood by a person on the street. At the risk of being redundant, I want to remind you of a quote from Pope Francis that I cited in chapter two:

> There are times when the faithful, in listening to completely orthodox language, take away something alien to the authentic Gospel of Jesus Christ, because that language is alien to their own way of speaking to and understanding one another. With

2. Benedict XVI, Encyclical on Christian Hope *Spe salvi*, nos. 41–44. www.vatican.va.

> the holy intent of communicating the truth about God and humanity, we sometimes give them a false god.[3]

If curiosity leads us to look up *permit* in a dictionary, we will find multiple meanings. The first entry will undoubtedly imply responsibility, and so we see that if a priest uses the term, even if it is used appropriately in a theological sense, the hearer is likely to receive an unintended message. God is made to look like the responsible party for evil.

It is important to explain this clearly and to find an alternate term to refer to God's position on moral evil, a term that may be more easily understood on the street. Perhaps it would be more appropriate, and more easily understood, to say that God loves or respects human freedom, but not that he permits evil. God forbids evil, but he endures it and is pained by it. He is a passive agent in a strict sense; he suffers evil.

Does a Mother "Permit" a Child to Suffer and Die?

The only sense in which perhaps we could affirm that God permits evil would be the sense that applies to a mother. Does a mother "permit" her child to suffer and die? A mother, when she brings a child into the world, knows that, throughout the course of his or her

3. Francis, *Evangelii gaudium*, no. 41.

life, that child will experience pain and will ultimately die. Why, then, bring a child into the world? Because a mother understands that while life is accompanied by suffering, it is inherently good. She does not desire suffering for her child; she desires to see her loved one happy and healthy.

The same is true of God: He desires our well-being. He specifically wants two overarching goods for his children: life and freedom. But he knows, as does a mother, that we will all one way or another have to face evil, pain, and suffering. God is not the one who sends pain and evil, however. We bring harm upon ourselves, especially in the case of moral evil.

If we were to say to a mother that she is "permitting" her child to suffer, she would be furious with us. Certainly, if we cannot say this to her—because this is not the case—we cannot say it to God, who loves us more than any earthly parent ever could.

V.

God and Natural Evil

Collateral Damage

We understand natural evil to be any occurrence in which human intervention or decisions do not play a role, such as floods, earthquakes, typhoons, accidents of any kind, and illnesses. Human freedom is not a hidden cause in any of these events. While we do suffer natural evils, we do nothing voluntarily to cause them.

With respect to previous generations, we have come a long way in our understanding of this type of harm. Earlier philosophers had little knowledge about certain aspects of nature that are now clear to us, which rendered them unable to find logical explanations for so many natural disasters.

From an objective point of view, the explanation for natural evil does not currently present a theological problem. It is simply a product of the complexity of the material world. This complexity means that any action (even our own human action), together with positive results, often brings additional, less positive, unintended consequences.

In military terms, such consequences are called "collateral damage." In medical terminology, they are "side effects." For example, a medicine that helps with a heart condition may cause stomach problems; a medicine for the stomach may damage the liver, and so on.

This is true in myriad areas of life. Several years ago, in Valencia, Spain, the famous Albufera (a large freshwater lagoon and wetland area) underwent fumigation. The effort was successful. Mosquitos disappeared (or were considerably reduced), along with the malaria endemic that had afflicted the zone. But subsequently, it was discovered that several species of birds that feed on mosquitoes had also disappeared.

An additional example—and perhaps one of the greatest paradigms—is the automobile. It is fair to say that automobiles were one of the most life-changing inventions, representing an incredible leap forward in mobility, productivity, and quality of life. Cars have been a great good for humanity; but nevertheless, every year more than one million people die in car accidents worldwide. Do these tragedies outweigh the benefits of car use? In this case, we cannot discard the valuable to spare the detrimental. Though we should certainly enact as many measures as possible to reduce the number of accident-related deaths, we cannot deny that automobiles have been one of the most impactful advances in history. The negative side effects do not outweigh the good caused by their invention.

The same is true of such inventions as the internet, mobile telephones, and electricity. All profound advances, they have each caused some negative side effects.

Likewise, even our good deeds can have some negative consequences, such as when an act of kindness is misinterpreted. Popular wisdom affirms that everything has its pros and cons. Most things in this world include positive and negative aspects alike.

With technological advances in mind, we also know for a fact that the so-called "natural evils" are all secondary consequences of several absolutely indispensable conditions for life on earth. We will look at several examples.

Life on earth would be impossible without rain. This is evident. And God created nature so that it rains regularly in almost every part of the world, in an authentically amazing balance. But every once in a while, in a specific place, it rains too little or it rains too much. These few exceptions to the norm are called "natural disasters," be they droughts or typhoons. But we cannot forget that these are the extreme ends on the spectrum that is the earth's incredible water cycle, absolutely essential for life.

Earthquakes? Any geologist can explain their critical function of maintaining stability in the earth's crust. If there were no earthquakes allowing the earth's crust to move, we could potentially come to a point where the whole planet would explode. And furthermore, we must realize that the great majority of earthquakes are no more than a soft tremor. They do their job practically unnoticed.

Without wind, there would be no rain, nor circulation of the air. And when the wind blows a little too hard, we call it a hurricane and we can get angry with God. But we fail to thank him on days (most days) in which the wind quietly brings us water and life. If the air were still, life as we know it would cease to exist.

More examples? Without viruses and bacteria, life as we know it would be impossible. Most viruses and bacteria are beneficial for human life. Without these good bacteria we would not have molecular life, marine plankton, or the processes of digestion, fermentation of foods, and decomposition.

In summary, any unbiased person with a minimal knowledge of nature should be motivated to praise God for his greatness and wisdom. Scientists sometimes speak of the "anthropic principle," which indicates that nature is oriented toward the existence of human life on earth. There are hundreds of factors, seemingly random, that make possible, or at least facilitate, human subsistence: from the degree to which the earth's axis is tilted to the fact that water does not shrink when frozen (as is the case with almost all elements) but expands. There are myriad factors that, if even slightly modified, would cause all life on earth to disappear.

God does not wish for, nor does he send any physical evil, any harm. God loves life. Air, water, and the geological, biological, and genetic richness of this world are all good and only good—regardless of whether these good gifts have unpleasant secondary effects.

Of course, this may offer little comfort to people who suffer a hurricane or other natural disaster. But if we stop to think things through carefully, we can come to no other conclusion than to acknowledge and praise God for his wisdom. I have spoken with people who have denied the wisdom of God on the basis of so much evil and pain in the world. My response is that if the evil that is present could cause us to deny God, how much more should the good around us lead us to affirm his existence. No matter which aspect of life we consider, it is undeniable that there is far more good than evil.

It is a mistake to give more attention to evil than to good. It may be human nature, but it is not a correct way of thinking. If we have a toothache, we may really be in agony, but should we forget to give glory to God and thank him for all of the other teeth (and so many other organs in the body) that are working perfectly? Natural evil should not cloud the beauty, grandeur, and goodness of creation!

The Unanswerable Question: Why Me?

In the previous section, we gave an overview of the complexity of the natural world and the logic for the existence of natural evil. But we should remember that any amount of explanation falls short when we personally face evil and pain. In the beginning of this book, we named C. S. Lewis as one of the authors who most clearly explained the problem of pain, and nevertheless, when his wife died, he sank into a deep depression. This is a clear example of how all the scientific explanations and statistics in the world are of little help when we are personally suffering.

When we experience a moral evil of human making, our first instinct is to find someone to blame. We can get angry, even react in hate and resentment, but there is normally someone we can hold responsible.

On the contrary, in the face of natural evil, there is no one who can be the direct object of our accusations and resentment. There is no easy explanation for why this has happened, and for most people, a big question arises: "Why me? Why do I have cancer? Why is my house sinking? Why was my child born with disabilities?" Many doubts about cause, purpose, and meaning are wrapped up in the question: "Why?"[1]

The answers do not come easily in daily life. Once, on a trip with a large group of friends, a person was struck by lightning. He survived with no other side effects than a few light burns, but the question naturally arose, "Why was I struck by lightning? Why not someone else?"

---

1. "Within each form of suffering endured by man, and at the same time at the basis of the whole world of suffering, there inevitably arises the question: *why?* It is a question about the cause, the reason, and equally, about the purpose of suffering, and, in brief, a question about its meaning. Not only does it accompany human suffering, but it seems even to determine its human content, what makes suffering precisely human suffering." John Paul II, *Salvifici doloris*, no. 9.

One of the best illustrations I have found is in an old joke:

> Two men are in a football stadium crowded with people, and one asks the other, "Do you know how many spectators fit in this stadium?"
>
> "Well, I'm not quite sure," answers the second. "I suppose about a hundred thousand."
>
> The first is quiet. Then he mutters, "One hundred thousand spectators! Twenty-two players! Two linesmen, and one referee! I don't get it!"
>
> A moment goes by in silence and then he says again, "One hundred thousand spectators! Twenty-two players! Two linesmen, and one referee! I don't get it!"
>
> "What's your point?" the other finally asks. "Do you think the stadium is too big, or what?"
>
> "Exactly! It's huge! Can you believe that, with so many people here, the blessed pigeon came to leave his present on *my* head!?"

This simple joke exposes an undeniable reality. A biologist could explain to this football fan why pigeons excrete their waste while flying, a physicist could talk about the force of gravity and air resistance, an ecologist could explain the existence of pigeons as a gift of nature and their place in the evolutionary tree, and an artist could tell him about the beauty of the pigeon and its flight. However, no expert—nor any person at all—could tell him why the pigeon droppings have fallen on his head and not on the head of the person sitting next to him.

When we are faced with pain produced by natural evil, asking "Why me?" will only help sink us deeper into despair and depression. It is a senseless question. People may laugh at that joke because everyone understands that it centers around a ridiculous question, and the absurdity makes us laugh. And yet, when we have problems, we sometimes ask this same question.

Moving on to a more serious explanation, Aristotle said that science cannot be applied to individual cases. To ask why is to question the causes, to search for a rational explanation, but science is not possible in isolated situations. And since irrational questions have no possible answers, it is therefore this rational impossibility that sinks us into despair and distress.

Some people, in an attempt to resolve the absurdity of the question "Why me?" have come to a simplistic answer: "This is what God wanted." In this way, they make God into the villain, the one who is to blame for their pain and suffering. And instead of thanking God for the existence of pigeons, with all their beauty and wonderful biology, they become angry with God and believe that he is the source of their problems.

Do Not Try to Explain the Unexplainable

Things get worse when pious, well-meaning people say something like, "You have to accept the will of God," or "God sends us sickness so that we draw closer to him."

These kinds of statements can provoke a person with genuine faith to reply, "Don't blame God! He does not send us problems!" It takes courage to admit that we do not know why a sickness has fallen on us and not on the next person.

There certainly could be a medical reason. But in many cases of physical pain, just as with natural disasters, there is no real answer as to why one person instead of another suffers the malady. And we should not involve God in our explanations in such a way that we make God seem responsible for our pain.

I was quite happy to learn that Pope John Paul II once visited a leper colony in India with the nuns of Mother Teresa of Calcutta. During this visit he spent time talking with the lepers and said, "I cannot explain why you suffer, but I can assure you that God loves you." Let us not try to explain the unexplainable! And by no means should we somehow make God to blame.

Pope Benedict XVI answered a few questions on the program *In His Image*, on RAI (Italian Public Television), broadcast in Rome on Good Friday, April 22, 2011.

"Holy Father," said the host,

> I want to thank you for your presence here, which fills us with joy and helps us remember that today is the day in which Jesus showed his love in the most radical way, that is, by dying on the Cross as an innocent.

The first question was precisely about the topic of innocent sorrow and came from a seven-year-old Japanese girl who said,

> My name is Elena. I am Japanese and I am seven years old. I am very frightened because the house where I felt safe really shook a lot and many children my age have died. I cannot go to play in the park. I want to know: why do I have to be so afraid? Why do children have to be so sad? I'm asking the Pope, who speaks with God, to explain it to me.

"Dear Elena," responded Benedict XVI,

> I send you my heartfelt greetings. I also have the same questions: why is it this way? Why do you have to suffer so much while others live in ease? And we do not have the answers but we know that Jesus suffered as you do, an innocent, and that the true God who is revealed in Jesus is by your side. This seems very important to me, even though we do not have answers, even if we are still sad; God is by your side and you can be certain that this will help you. One day we will even understand why it was so. At this moment it seems important to me that you know "God loves me" even if it seems he doesn't know me.[2]

---

2. Interview with His Holiness Benedict XVI on the TV Program "In His Image, Questions on Jesus," *L'Osservatore Romano*, Weekly Edition (April 27, 2011). www.vatican.va.

In part two of this book, I will suggest how we should react when faced with pain, but for now it is important to highlight the teachings of these two great pontiffs, with all their authority: We do not have an answer; we cannot give an explanation. Nor should we attempt to explain the unexplainable. We should have the courage to say that we do not know.

When someone in distress approaches us with the question "Why me?" we must explain that this is an unanswerable question. We should lovingly say that the question to be asked is something else, a different question. We will discuss this in the final chapters.

The Autonomy of This World

If an earthquake comes and people die, is God not to blame?

We are going to answer this with a historical anecdote, although it may be more myth than fact. In 1687, Isaac Newton published his key work, *Philosophiæ Naturalis Principia Mathematica*, in which he described the laws of planetary movement and the universal law of gravity, among other things. It is said that Newton was later invited to the court of the king of France to present and explain the *Principia*. After the exposition, the king asked him:

> "And in all of this theory, where do we find God?"
>
> "Your Majesty," responded Newton, "in my theory, God is an unnecessary hypothesis."

It is probably more fiction than fact, because it does not seem like Newton to give such a simple answer. But it is interesting. Until Newton, the general belief was that if the planets, the sun, and the moon were in motion, it was because God was guiding them with his finger. Newton explained that this is not so; planets revolve around their orbits as proposed by Copernicus, following the laws of Kepler that had recently been discovered. They do not move because God is pushing them, but because they follow the universal law of gravity.

And Newton was right; God is not essential to explain the movements of the planets—only their existence, and the existence of the very law of gravity.

God brings forth creation out of nothing; he sets it in motion and leaves it working according to his design through immutable laws, some of which humans have discovered along the way, such as gravity. God is not moving the planets with his finger. Neither is he unleashing hurricanes, earthquakes, or lightning strikes that spark wildfires; nor is he sending viruses into our bodies. God set all of creation spinning, in an incredibly miraculous way, with a precise equilibrium that makes life on earth possible. As we have seen, the goods that shape our world sometimes have extreme secondary effects that end up being detrimental. But we can never say that a hurricane or wildfire is the result of a direct action of God, or that it was God who made us sick. God is never the cause of evil.

This is the principle of the autonomy of creation.

Providence and Evil

To talk about the providence of God is almost synonymous with speaking about God himself. No providence exists apart from God. In summary, we can define providence as the loving care of God in all things.[3]

Regarding the problem of evil, the issue is that some postures focused excessively on providence have led us to burden the concept with ideas that cannot be logically attributed to Divine Providence. I will explain this with a literary anecdote.

Giovanni Guareschi was an Italian writer known for a series of books published in the 1950s about the life and adventures of a small-town priest named Don Camillo. His interactions with the communist mayor Peppone became famous worldwide, and the story made its way onto cinema screens. In the Don Camillo books, one of the prominent characters is a Christ figure, a large crucifix on the high altar. Don Camillo talks quite naturally with Christ, who frequently responds.

In the first book, a chapter entitled "The Bell" describes Don Camillo's struggles as he tries to raise funds with which to buy a bell to replace the old one called Gertrudis. Gertrudis had been stolen by Germans during the Second World War and Don Camillo is anxious to put another in its place. After several exploits, a rich old lady in the town named Signora Carolina has a successful enterprise and decides to give

---

3. *Catechism of the Catholic Church*, no. 302.

the money she earned toward the purchase of the new bell. Wildly happy, Don Camillo tells Christ what has happened. The priest says he will buy a large candle to put at the feet of Christ in demonstration of his gratitude. When he starts to run off to buy the candle, Christ calls him. Here is the conversation that follows:

"No candle, Don Camillo," Christ said severely. "No candle."

"But why?"

"Because I do not deserve it," replied Christ.

> I have given the Signora Carolina no help of any kind in her affairs. If I were to intervene in such matters, the winner would bless Me while the loser would justifiably curse Me. If you happen to find a purse of money, I have not made you find it, because I did not cause your neighbor to lose it. You had better light your candle in front of the middleman who helped the Signora Carolina make a profit of nine million. I am no middleman.[4]

On occasion, I have heard people say, "I do not believe in coincidences, only providence." Although this statement represents a profound supernatural vision, it is still a dangerous assumption. If everything were a direct result of providence, then any event could be attributed to providence, including accidents, sicknesses, fires, or floods. In conclusion, providence would be responsible

---

4. Giovanni Guareschi, *The Little World of Don Camillo*, trans. Una Vincenzo Troubridge (Gollancz, 1951).

for the harm we suffer. But this is not true; providence neither causes accidents, nor is it responsible for business gains or losses, as Guareschi writes.

The issue centers on a correct understanding of what providence entails. Allow me to briefly clarify.

In the previous chapter, we discussed the autonomy of creation and used the example of planetary movement. Where do we find God? Where is providence? The answer is that God is revealed in the very existence of the planets (of the whole universe, actually). Furthermore, he is not just revealed in creation, but also in the conservation of its existence, together with all the natural laws that make its continuation possible.

But, as we have explained, God is not dragging the planets along with his fingertip. God creates and preserves the world and has given each created being the ability to act according to its own nature. He lets each act in freedom. This freedom in humans is freedom of decision, freedom to construct their own lives. Taking into account the complexity of the material world, less intelligent beings have autonomy to function according to their natures, but not freedom.

But neither God nor his providence are directly responsible for our actions, just as they do not expressly bring about any accident that we may have. As we have seen before, any physical harm we experience is a side effect of greater good.

In other words, God's providence is behind every being and every occurrence, but is not dictating their actions step by step; rather, he is only making possible that a being exists and is able to act according to its specific way of being.[5]

It is good to ask God to help us to understand him and his loving care. One of the most important statements in the Gospels, and perhaps one of the least understood, is the answer that Jesus gives to the Pharisees when they ask him if the kingdom of God is coming. Jesus answers, "The kingdom of God is in the midst of you" (Lk 17:21). And on top of that, when Pilate accuses him, asking if he is the king, Jesus answers, "My kingship is not of this world" (Jn 18:36).

God acts primarily in the soul of each human being. But he is not responsible for the tragedies that befall us, the injustices we experience, nor the illnesses we contract. What he is concerned with, in his grace, is that we bear well the burdens caused by tragedies, injustices, and sicknesses. Here yes, the grace of God is directly at work, helping us to respond well internally, not to get angry or lose hope.

The kingdom of God works from within us, by the grace of God through the action of the Holy Spirit. It is visible in our words and actions. Yet we, by excessively declaring circumstances to be providential,

---

5. The study of providence exceeds the limits of this book. To go deeper into this topic, read St. Thomas Aquinas, *Summa Theologiae*, 1.22. Aquinas specifies that providence acts in all created beings. But this action is through the beings themselves. In the case of humans, our freedom means that we decide and do everything in liberty. There is a universal providence of God behind each of our actions, but not an express desire of God. The decision is ours, not God's. What God wants is that we be free and, therefore, responsible for our actions.

seem determined to hold God responsible for external affairs. The Church has condemned various "messianisms" that have shown up over the years. These are always a product of people insisting on mixing up God with earthly happenings, making God an excuse for our own interests, a pretext to declare war or excuse injustices. When we place responsibility on God for external happenings, something becomes irreversibly twisted. And then, with our comments, we can open the door for people to curse the name of God, whom we have held responsible for whatever befalls us.

Everything mentioned above, when rightly understood, does not negate the possibility that exceptional events may occur if God so desires. No man can attempt to put God in a box. When God decides to act, he does, and no one can demand an explanation. But in this book, we are aiming to study ordinary events of daily life, not the rare exceptions, the miracles that take place when God wishes. It is evident that God can perform miracles, and he has. But it is also clear that everyday life happens independently of what we consider to be "miracles."

Providence or Coincidence?

So then, is there no such thing as providence, only mere coincidence? Not exactly. Miracles aside, God in his grace works on the inside, directly in the heart of a person. And outside is the realm of material complexity and, from our point of view, coincidence.

Let us dig a little deeper. Any event here on earth is a result of something that has caused it. When the cause is immediate and clear, we can study it and see the relationship with the consequence. We can observe what happens when one billiard ball bumps into another, what happens when I ignite gunpowder, and what happens if the oil in a motor runs out.

But there are many other occurrences that are not the result of one concrete action, but rather a nearly infinite, never-ending string of causes. Let us consider, for example, a car crash involving two cars colliding in a busy intersection. For this to have happened, a long list of causes must have coincided—causes such as the quality of each driver's sleep the night before, the time the drivers left home that day or night, the delay caused by one of their children; the fact that one driver was a little distracted at the time of the accident, that a car that caused a visual obstruction was parked on that particular street and not on another. There are multiple factors, including many that depend on human freedom, such as one person deciding to buy a car and not a motorcycle, the mothers of both drivers deciding to have a child, the reason for each driver being in the location where the accident took place. Additionally, a mathematical principle called "chaos theory" comes into play: Tiny causes that have nonlinear consequences infinitely complicate the situation.

These situations, which are impossible to explain with any singular cause, are known as coincidences. And life is full of them. What all coincidences have in common is that no one can identify one determining cause. This is reflected in the story of the pigeon. We will never be able to find out why its droppings fell on one person and not on another nearby. It was a coincidence.

We cannot hold God responsible. Perhaps a person thinks, "Since God knows everything, he controls the infinite series of causes and made the droppings fall on my head." No, we are not God's puppets. In the first place, God does not guide the pigeon with his finger, just as he does not steer the planets. Furthermore, the man found himself in the stadium because he wanted to be there, because he freely decided to go to a game and to sit where he was sitting. In any accident (in any natural evil that happens) our own free actions play a role, and we are the only ones responsible for these.

Let's look at another example: If, as I am leaving my house, a shingle falls on my head, it must have fallen because it was improperly attached (the free action of the human who built the roof). Furthermore, I left my house at that time after having woken up, gotten dressed, brushed my teeth, organized the house, and cared for the children. Any slight variation in my free actions, even of a fraction of a second, would have resulted in the shingle not hitting me when it fell.

So how can coincidences and natural evils even relate to God? God works in souls and, through those souls, in the world. Words from a priest, the example of a friend, the help someone can give me in an opportune moment, or something I might read can all help me to discover the love of God and stir my soul. In the same way, any natural event, such as a sickness, can lead me to reflect and to turn my thoughts to God. This is another manifestation of providence working in my heart, at times through an external event. But ordinarily, this external event is not initiated by providence. What providence does is take advantage of external circumstances so that the grace of God can stir our souls and lead us to an internal conversion.

Providence can act in a thousand ways in this world but is always oriented principally toward the growth of the kingdom of God in the inner hearts of human beings.

Blessed Complexity

At the beginning of this chapter, we saw that natural evil is intrinsically related to the complexity of the material world. Because of this complexity, many causes have both good and bad effects.

Why must the world be so complex? Could it have all been simpler?

The complexity of the natural world is analogous to the principle of human freedom and moral evil. Without free will, there would be no moral evil; and without complexity in nature, there would be no natural evil. But just as freedom is necessary for humans to exist and to be able to love, so is complexity intrinsically necessary for the existence of the material world. Complexity not only allows for creation to exist, but also for it to develop into a nearly infinite variety of life forms unique to the planet Earth.

Without complexity, there would be no diversity and no beauty. Without complexity, there would be no individuality; we would all be clones of one another. Without complexity, we would not have landscapes, sunsets reflected in the clouds, or the rustling of leaves in the breeze. It would all be a uniform wasteland. Literature, art, and laughter would cease to exist.

In summary, if freedom is a great gift of God for intelligent human beings, then complexity is the great gift of God for the material world. Complexity fills the world with life, diversity, and beauty—even though it can have some negative side effects, just as freedom inevitably may be used for evil. Nevertheless, both freedom and complexity are good gifts for which we should constantly thank God.

VI.

A Few Specific Questions

The Asymmetry of Good and Evil

I was once asked, "You say that all good comes from God. So then, how is it that all evil does not also come from God?"

This question is valid. To respond we will now take a look at what is known as the asymmetry of good and evil.

In the Nobel Prize award ceremony, the winners give a brief speech. Usually, the winners thank those who helped them to reach this point, and it is not uncommon for them to take the opportunity to thank their parents. Nevertheless, their parents may very well have been uneducated persons who couldn't read or write. Even so, to acknowledge them makes sense: The winner owes them everything; without parents, he or she would never have been born, and may never have had the opportunities that led to notable accomplishments.

There is a clear asymmetry in the consequences of good and evil. We can in some way thank God for any good that happens to us, although he may not have had anything to do with it directly. For example, if a friend gives me a birthday present, it is fair to thank the friend, but it is also fair to thank God. Without God creating the world and bringing us into it, there would be no friend, no world to live in, and no gifts to be given.

Therefore, with things that are good, it is strictly true that "everything is providence," since behind any good is the creative will of God, who has brought these good things into existence.[1] Without God, nothing would exist. Every good thing is an ultimate consequence of the creative will of God. Although my friend decides to give me a gift out of his own free will, I can thank God for my friend's existence, for his freedom, and for his ability to make this decision.

On the contrary, no bad thing that happens can be traced back to God. The winner of the Nobel Prize has good reason to be grateful to his parents. But if his wallet is stolen, if he becomes sick, or if he has a car accident, it would be ridiculous to blame his parents. This is the asymmetry of good and evil. His parents wanted him to live a good life, and they set him on the path to grow and gain knowledge. They did not intend or provide for their child to suffer a theft, a sickness, or an accident.

God, through a long chain of intermediary causes, is ultimately responsible for good, but the only person responsible for evil is the person who has carried it out. It would be ridiculous to prosecute the grandparents

---

1. Additionally, in the case of good actions that involve supernatural merit, the doctrine of the Church is that human freedom always needs the help of divine grace. In this sense, with greater reason, we can attribute them to the providence of God, together with human will.

of a murderer simply because of their genetic association to their grandchild.

The asymmetry between good and evil is not a rhetorical strategy to thank God for good and acquit him from the bad. It stems from the very nature of good and evil.

Without delving into too many philosophical rabbit holes, I will point out that good is always constructive. The author of a good deed constructs something and is henceforth co-responsible for the resulting good. The previous example is most clear: Parents, by bringing a child into the world, give the unsurpassable gift of life; good that the child does in his or her life can point back to the parents if their influence has been positive and a good in itself.

Evil, on the contrary, is by its nature destructive. When something is totally destroyed, the effects logically end with what has been destroyed. Precisely because what has been destroyed no longer exists, it cannot be the cause of any subsequent effects. If a murderer kills a twelve-year-old boy, the deceased child's life has ended; he cannot do anything else. There are no further effects, good or bad. The consequences of the evil end with the destroyed life. By killing this child, the murderer cut off all future possibilities. Had the child lived, he may have grown up to be an engineer or a doctor. He may have gotten married and had children; no one knows. Any possible future is hypothetical and unreal; we have no way of knowing what could have evolved in his life.

There may be negative consequences by omission, but they will never be something real, something tangible, only aborted possibilities. This is already a lot: For this reason, evil is malignant; it is destructive but it ceases to be the direct cause of other effects, good or evil. Good, in contrast, having given birth to something, continues to work through this new thing that has come into being.

This is not only true in the case of new life. Think of someone who builds a house, starts a company, or founds an association. Even after that person dies, these entities (these good things) once begun, can continue to exist for many years to come, bringing good to countless other people.

From a metaphysical point of view, this asymmetry is reflected in the substantial inequality between good and evil. They are not equal and opposite concepts. They are completely unequal and belong to two separate categories of being. Good has an entity in its own right and evil does not. They cannot be placed on either end of a balance and weighed. The comparison makes no sense. Essentially, evil is destructive and good is constructive. Their fruits cannot be compared.

In practice, it may seem that evil abounds and has a much larger impact than good. But it is a question of impact. Good creates and leads created beings toward their perfection, toward the intention the Creator has for them. Not so with evil, which does not create anything, but only deforms and hinders creatures from reaching their purpose.

With this perspective, we understand that the providence of God is behind any created good and sustains the good actions of free creatures. But the same cannot be said of evil actions. All good definitely comes from God, but God never wills, nor helps, nor sustains evil. Divine Providence is *asymmetrical.*

This asymmetry is reason for us to have a radical optimism about the flourishing of humanity. Good is always constructive, and what is constructed remains. Evil destroys. It does not construct anything that lasts, and for this reason, evil always ends up destroying itself. The clearest example is the antithesis of peace and war. The world could live permanently in peace for millennia. Nothing would stop it. On the contrary, permanent war is impossible. Sooner or later, the contenders wear out, the soldiers die off or get tired of fighting, support for the conflict ends. It is impossible for evil to last long term. Good, in contrast, endures.

It is true that evil persists in the heart of humans. When one evil is stopped, another will soon follow, but none of these evils will last for long. All the while, the good slowly, little by little, improves the world and will continue to make it a better place.

Couldn't God Have Created a Better World?

You may agree that God wants only what is good and does not send us evil. But couldn't he have made things to be a bit simpler? Couldn't he have created a world without evil? Couldn't he have made a better version of the world?

This is a question as old as time. Since the time this question was raised many centuries ago, myriad responses have come forth. At the end of the day, it does not cease to be a rhetorical question, with almost no practical impact for today's world. It does us no good to waste time thinking about hypotheticals: What could have been but wasn't and will never be. What would life be like if, instead of being born in Spain, I had been born in Alaska? Nobody knows. But this is of very little consequence to my actual life.

All the same, since this question can leave open the possibility of us blaming God for our problems, it would be beneficial to find an answer, even though that answer may be incomplete.

The best answer is found in our own incompetence as stewards. Any time we set out to modify the blueprints of nature, we only succeed in making a bigger mess. Certainly, we have built highways, ships, planes and hundred-story buildings, but all of this has been constructed (more or less) within the bounds of nature. When we try to go against nature—by deforestation, overconsumption of resources, and pollution, for example—what we achieve is the destruction of the environment and the elimination of many living species.

We were created to live on earth as stewards of God's handiwork, respecting and caring for nature. Each time we try to change what God has made, without regard for the design code, there are negative consequences. Think, for example, of contaminated rivers and seas, the desertification of large areas, the disappearance of fauna and flora, or climate change.

Humans have been able to remediate certain problems (through advances in medical, scientific, and environmental knowledge) and promote some good. Nonetheless, God's creation is above reproach. When someone begins to criticize God's creation, we might ask, "Could you have made it better?"

Our task is to care for creation and to help one another to the best of our ability, using all the gifts and knowledge God has provided. There will always be evil and mistakes but, working together, we can improve many things. We should not forget that God has left the world in our hands and calls us to participate in the perfection of creation. When problems arise, they do not have so much to do with God as with us, because we failed to understand how to care for the world that God entrusted to us.[2]

Modern science also serves to demonstrate the incredible beauty, complexity, and balance of this world. How many subatomic particles exist? More than two hundred subatomic particles have been detected, which include neutrons, protons, electrons, positrons, photons, and the more recently discovered quarks, bosons, mesons, and baryons.

---

2. Francis, Encyclical Letter on Care for Our Common Home *Laudato si'* (May 24, 2015). www.vatican.va. The entire encyclical is a defense of ecology correctly understood, and an exhortation to care for nature and avoid unjustified impacts.

According to the latest theories, all these particles can be reduced to three extremely elemental particles: quarks, leptons, and bosons. Moreover, if we go a little deeper, the hypothesis is that even these particles can be reduced to condensed energy in different forms. And with just this one element known as energy, God has created the entire universe, with all its stars, planets, oceans, mountains, plants, animals, and people—millions and millions of people, each one unique.

Is there any human being who could have done a better job?

"Irremediable" Evils

There is one last question that we cannot neglect. Sometimes, there is no possible remedy for the evil we have created.

Humans are experts at blaming others. Further, when we find ourselves in a horrible situation with no apparent way out, we are sometimes tempted to blame God.

Case in point: Several years ago in 2021, it was reported that an eleven-year-old girl in Bolivia became pregnant as the result of a rape. Automatically, people raised complaints because the Church would not "authorize" the girl to have an abortion.

This reaction brought to light a great hypocrisy. Instead of focusing blame on the sex offender, the parents who did not adequately take care of their daughter, or the lack of public safety measures, many people blamed God and the Church.

We find it difficult to admit that certain situations, such as this one, have no ideal solution. An abortion would destroy human life, a clear violation of the sixth commandment. Continuation of the pregnancy would pose extreme and unpredictable difficulties for the girl, already suffering as the victim of abuse. There was no satisfactory solution, save a miracle. Now, free will allows each of us to do what we wish and what our conscience allows, but we cannot force nor expect God to perform a miracle to solve a problem that we (or others) have created. Is anger at God justified, for evils that humans have caused?

Not long ago, the question arose of what to do with frozen embryos (millions!), a product of in vitro fertilization technology and of medical experiments. Yet again, the dilemma was presented to the Church as if it were the Church's problem. The Church had warned long ago about this issue, consistently denying the legitimacy of in vitro fertilization, partly because of the question of what to do with the embryos not implanted. But when the problem came to a head, some people tried to push the responsibility of finding a solution onto the Church.

It seems horrible to leave embryos frozen for centuries. The longer they are frozen, the lower their viability is. Terminating their existence is repugnant to both reason and emotion. And obligating millions of women to become surrogates to save the embryos goes against common sense and is not feasible. So then, what can be done? What is the solution?

No matter the solution, it will harm someone. In this circumstance, where embryos have been forced to exist outside the womb, there is no feasible solution that will fit within the bounds of morality. The Church has been commanded by Christ to uphold Christ's teachings and help her members live in love. She cannot—and should never be expected to—teach against this mission any more than God can go against his goodness.

We should be brave enough to own our errors and recognize that often there is no solution. Good and evil have consequences that sometimes follow us for the rest of our lives.

Why Doesn't God Take the Pain Away?

Even if you agree with everything I have written so far, you may be wondering: Why doesn't God take away my pain? Isn't he omnipotent? Couldn't he take it away if he wanted?

This question can be answered with a quote from a historical novel entitled *Byzantium* by Stephen Lawhead. When the protagonist, Aidan—a priest who has suffered much—complains to his superior in the convent that God has not done anything to alleviate his suffering, he receives this reply:

> As He did nothing when His beloved son died on the cross. . . . We are closest to Christ when

> sharing the world's misery. [Did you think] Jesus came to remove our pains? Wherever did you get that notion? The Lord came, not to remove our suffering, but to show us the way through it to the glory beyond. We can overcome our travails. That is the promise of the cross.[3]

God can work miracles, but it is not logical for us to insist that he do so. We may ask for a miracle but not demand one. However, it is not unusual to find people who are angry with God, not because he sent them suffering, but because he did nothing to take it away.

We must remember, as Lawhead wrote, that Jesus came to earth not to remove evil from our bodies but to heal our souls. Divine Providence acts primarily in the inner soul, not to cure the body (miracles notwithstanding). As we have seen, although it is difficult to understand and accept, Jesus said that "the kingdom of God is in the midst of you" (Lk 17:21). It is in the midst of us—not outside us, not in physical illness, not in economic crises, not in the injustice someone may commit against us.

So then, can we pray that God take away sickness or any other trial? Yes, we can pray and ask; and it is always good to pray, to ask God to take away our pain, but under two conditions.

The first is to not forget what we say in the Lord's Prayer: "Thy will be done." Sometimes, by the way we

---

3. Stephen R. Lawhead, *Byzantium* (HarperCollins, 1996), p. 610.

react when God does not do what we ask, it seems as though we have prayed, "You must do *my* will. And if you do not, I will be upset." This is no way to pray. A miracle is a free gift that we can ask for, but to which we are in no way entitled. We may ask for whatever we want, trusting in God and in his wisdom, but we should never make demands or get angry when our petition is not granted.

The second and most important condition is that while we can ask for the pain to go away, we should more earnestly ask that God help us to sanctify it. The things of this world are temporary, as is the pain. It may be important that we are freed from our pain, but more important still is that we know how to make sense of it and use the experience to grow closer to God and gain heaven. In part two of this book, we will explore how to do this.

Keeping in mind these two conditions, the prayer of petition is good and pleasing to God. There are many passages in the Gospels in which Jesus encourages us to pray and make our requests with boldness.

But we must have a clear understanding of faith and Christian religion, and of the value of prayer—especially the prayer of petition, with which we request the intervention of Divine Providence. When we experience an illness or another type of difficulty and we come to God to ask for healing, a few things may happen.

First, God may respond with an extraordinary miracle. This is called the *extraordinary providence* of God. This can happen if God wills and as he decides.

The second possible outcome is that we are treated by a doctor and are cured, or, at the very least, have the pain alleviated. This fits into the *ordinary providence* of God. Without the necessity of extraordinary miracles, God works through everyday means. His intervention may go unnoticed, but he helps the doctor to determine the correct treatment, makes the medicine to be effective, and so on. In other cases, God may help the perfect solution to arrive in time to resolve a distressing situation. He may send an intermediary to work out a serious family conflict or soften a person's heart so that he or she makes a generous donation, or a thousand other things.

This is the way Divine Providence most frequently works, and we should be humble enough to admit that we will not know, until we reach heaven, to what extent our prayers have determined the outcome of a problem. Furthermore, we should not sit idly by, but, by every means available, work to find a solution.

And finally, if healing never comes, it does not mean that God has not heard us or that his providence has failed. It means that, for the time being, the circumstances must follow their natural course, and it is not in our best interest that they change. In this case, we may ask: Is my prayer ineffective? Absolutely not. Our prayers have served to increase our faith and trust in God and many times have helped us to carry the burden with a more patient and supernatural vision.

Prayer is always effective, although at times not in the way we would like. The very act of prayer in and of itself already has great supernatural value and gives us a heavenly perspective.

We cannot expect the Lord to take away all our pain and suffering. It is true that Jesus healed many while on earth, but this was an extraordinary time. It was essential for the people listening to understand that he was not just another man, another teacher. The miracles of Jesus had the primary purpose of bringing people to faith in the divinity of Christ.

The purpose of Jesus's life on earth was not to take away all pain, but rather to show us the way to heaven. If we become angry with God because he does not remove our suffering, we deserve to be asked the question previously cited: "[Did you think] Jesus came to remove our pains? Wherever did you get that notion?" How important that we as Christians accept that "the Lord came, not to remove our suffering, but to show us the way through it to the glory beyond."[4]

4. Lawhead, *Byzantium*, p. 610.

Part II

Face-to-Face with Pain

VII.

How to Deal with Pain?

So far, we have explained that God does not wish any evil, only good. He does not "permit" evil (in the colloquial use of the word), but he does want two great goods: human freedom and the existence of the material world in all its beauty and complexity.

When asked if God permits moral evil, such as murder or war, we must say that the answer is no, that God loves freedom and accepts its consequences but strictly prohibits any kind of evil action. If we carry out evil, it is our action, not God's.

Similarly, anytime we face a natural evil we must affirm the creative will of God (reflected in the entire universe), which brings into being a wonderfully perfect natural world, and all the same accepts the inconvenient side effects that are a byproduct of the material world's complexity.

But now, from an existential point of view, we must take on the most important issue with the problem of pain: How should we react when we face suffering that affects us personally?

When we experience suffering, theoretical explanations fall short. A good start (great, actually) is to keep our head clear enough to not accuse God of causing our problems. But we also need to know how to deal with pain when the time comes.

Pain Is Not a Punishment from God

Before we go any further, we must address some commonly held misconceptions. The first is to see pain in some way as a punishment from God.

While many believers know that God does not punish us, no small number of Christians continue to view God through the lens of the Old Testament: If I do not obey, God will punish me. In fact, when a child gets hurt doing something he or she knew was wrong, it is not uncommon for a nearby adult to say, "You asked for it!," the insinuation being that God is punishing you.

These types of comments, deeply mistaken, can instill into the child's thinking that God punishes us, which is not true. This lie contributes to false beliefs about God.

God sends us good, not evil. He does not "punish" us with pain and suffering. An illness, for example, is never a punishment from God, and we should not blame him for it. The Book of Wisdom says, "God did not make death, and he does not delight in the death of the living" (Wis 1:13). God is not a God of death, but of life, happiness, and joy.

This perspective is unique to Christianity. For the Israelites in the time of Jesus, if a man were rich and successful, it was because God was on his side and gave him wealth. On the contrary, if a person were sick or broke, it was because he had sinned and God had punished him.

In the Gospels, Jesus sets things straight and explains this error in at least two significant texts. The first is found in the Gospel of Luke:

> There were some present at that very time who told him of the Galileans whose blood Pilate had mingled with their sacrifices. And he answered them, "Do you think that these Galileans were worse sinners than all the other Galileans, because they suffered thus? I tell you, No; but unless you repent you will all likewise perish. Or those eighteen upon whom the tower in Silo'am fell and killed them, do you think that they were worse offenders than all the others who dwelt in Jerusalem? I tell you, No; but unless you repent you will all likewise perish." (Lk 13:1–5)

Jesus makes clear that pain and misfortune are never a punishment from God for our sins. God does not punish us on this earth. There is no such thing as a "miracle" that brings harm. It is a very different thing when our own actions come back to bite us. A man who gets drunk frequently can end up losing his job, being kicked out of his house by his wife, and finding himself on the street with nowhere to go and without a cent in his pocket. But he has no one to blame other than himself. His own decisions have had negative consequences.

Jesus's words "but unless you repent you will all likewise perish," refer directly to the next life. "Perish" is not about death in this world, but about eternal death, separation from God.

Let's look at another passage, this time from the Gospel of John:

> As he passed by, he saw a man blind from his birth. And his disciples asked him, "Rabbi, who sinned, this man or his parents, that he was born blind?" Jesus answered, "It was not that this man sinned, or his parents, but that the works of God might be made manifest in him." (Jn 9:1–3)

Jesus subsequently performed a miracle, giving the man his sight back, but the key point is that the blindness was not a consequence of any sin, nor was it being used as a punishment. God sends us good, not evil.

Neither Is Pain a "Gift" from God

As we have seen, Jesus himself said that suffering is not a punishment from God. So then, according to an extremely "providentialist" way of thinking, it must be a gift from God.

No! We cannot think that a father would give a son, whom he passionately loves, pain. To suppose this would be crazy.

This misunderstanding has its origins in the different types of languages we discussed in chapter two, specifically in the gap between pious language and everyday language. To view a sickness or any other hardship as a demonstration of God's will may bring comfort and peace to a religious person.[1] But we should never imply that an illness forms part of God's will, unless we know with certainty that the listener understands the pious context of our words and will not be inclined to blame God for the hardship.

In today's society, very few people have the spiritual background necessary to understand the pious connotations of these sorts of comments. When the average person hears that sickness is a gift from God, he or she may not understand and may likely end up angry with the God who, according to what has been said, gives sickness as a "gift."

This is incorrect thinking, for pain is not a gift from God. To wish for or carry out evil is a sin, and God does not sin. God has not put into place one set of commands for us and another for himself. God cannot lie, steal, or be unfaithful. He cannot kill, injure, or make someone sick. God is all good, and only good. Sin is against his nature.

The Ten Commandments are not arbitrary. God does not change his commands from one day to the

---

1. Logically, if this idea fills us with peace, it is because, in some way, there is a relationship between what happens to us and the will of God. We will study this more carefully in the last chapter, in the section "Loving God's Will."

next and declare that we can now steal or kill. The commandments reflect the eternal nature of God, and we can even discover them through natural law. Even if God had not given Moses the Ten Commandments, it would still be wrong to steal, to lie, or to kill. God does not contradict himself. He is, as we have seen before, infinitely coherent.

Neither does it seem just that God would send us a natural evil for the purpose of bringing about a moral good. One permanent moral law is that the end never justifies the means. We cannot do evil to cause good. We cannot voluntarily harm someone just to obtain a positive result. For an action to be morally acceptable, both the act itself and the end goal must be good. God is never guilty of doing evil, not even to bring about something good.

The Fight Against Pain and Misery

When we find ourselves immersed in any kind of pain, whether it be sickness, injustice, or the death of a loved one, how should we respond? What does God expect us to do?

The answer is clear. It is the express will of God that we fight against evil, against pain, and against suffering. God wants us to defend life and well-being. This is yet another proof that God is never the cause of pain and evil. If sickness were directly willed by God, it would be a sin to go to the doctor. A traditional definition of sin is, precisely, to act against God's will.

On the contrary, God expects us to fight evil in all its forms. We should work to eliminate, together with evil, the pain and suffering that are side-effects of evil. This is true at every level: physical pain resulting from sickness, any type of injustice, world hunger, underdevelopment, sadness, or the effects of a natural disaster.

At the start of the new millennium, Pope John Paul II, at the World Youth Day prayer vigil in Rome, challenged young people with the following words:

> Today you have come together to declare that in the new century you will not let yourselves be made into tools of violence and destruction; you will defend peace, paying the price in your person if need be. You will not resign yourselves to a world where other human beings die of hunger, remain illiterate and have no work. You will defend life at every moment of its development; you will strive with all your strength to make this earth ever more livable for all people. Dear young people of the century now beginning, in saying "yes" to Christ, you say "yes" to all your noblest ideals.[2]

In summary, we are called to fight against evil, against pain and misery. If we are not committed to this cause, we cannot consider ourselves to be coherent Christians.

---

2. John Paul II, Address at the Vigil of Prayer (August 19, 2000). www.vatican.va.

In his letter *The Joy of the Gospel,* Pope Francis repeatedly encourages us to be concerned for others, especially for the neediest, for those who suffer, for anyone having a hard time.

How should we respond to pain? By fighting against it. In the case of our own pain, we fight by going to the doctor or by looking for a solution to the problem. God wants us to defend our well-being and our lives. If others are in pain, we fight by letting compassion take over and responding with solidarity and sensitivity, helping in whatever way possible. This is the Christian spirit; this is what God expects of us whenever we are confronted with pain. St. Josemaría Escrivá writes, "Do not pass by a neighbor's affliction with indifference. That person—a relative, a friend, a colleague . . . someone you don't know—is your brother."[3]

Here I would like to mention a special kind of struggle: when the evil comes not from without, but from within. If we are honest, we know that many times we are the principal agents of evil. Sometimes inadvertently, other times in error, we do things that are wrong and cause pain for others and for ourselves. Many times, we are aware of our errors: We are overcome by pride, envy, laziness, or any other inclination that comes from within and leads us astray. To engage in the fight against evil requires that we look inward and force ourselves to work to eradicate our bad attitudes and bad habits.

---

3. Josemaría Escrivá, *Furrow*, no. 251, in *The Way*, *Furrow*, *The Forge* (Scepter, 2004).

How can I fight against the evil that lies deep in my heart? How can I combat my own bad temper, my pride or impatience? The fight begins with acknowledging the evil inside of us. We must admit our own faults. This step alone is not easy. You will see how difficult it is for us! But without this step there is no way forward.

The next step is to completely reject it. For Christians, this is called repentance. C. S. Lewis writes:

> [Repentance] means unlearning all the self-conceit and self-will that we have been training ourselves in for thousands of years. It means killing a part of yourself, undergoing a kind of death. In fact, it needs a good man to repent.[4]

With this paradox so characteristic of Lewis, he brings our attention to a great truth: The further we sink into sin, the harder it is to repent. Only true repentance is capable of purifying our hearts and giving us strength to fight against evil.

Finally, our repentance should also be demonstrated in an effort to fix the mistakes we have made. To sincerely repent of having stolen something will lead us to return what was stolen. The same is true of any other harm. We should attempt to mitigate the damage we have caused. This same genuine repentance should lead us to ask for forgiveness from whomever we have harmed and from God, if we are people of faith. For

---

4. C. S. Lewis, *Mere Christianity* (HarperCollins, 1952), p. 56.

Christians, frequent confession of sins is a clear indication of our determination to fight against evil.

In short, this is objective proof that our conscience is sincere. We might rant about all that is wrong in politics, at work, or in our family, and all the while never make any effort to correct our own faults. If we never truly set out to change, to try to overcome (even if only with partial success) the evil inside of ourselves, any complaint against the evil and pain in the world will always be hypocrisy.

It will be helpful to remember Jesus's well-known words:

> For from within, out of the heart of man, come evil thoughts, fornication, theft, murder, adultery, coveting, wickedness, deceit, licentiousness, envy, slander, pride, foolishness. All these evil things come from within, and they defile a man. (Mk 7:21–23)

Any moral evil, any harm carried out by one person against another, has its root in the heart of the person. The fight against evil, if genuine, cannot overlook the evil that comes from within.

Overcome Evil with Good: Forgiveness

If we want to have a proper response when confronted with pain, another non-negotiable requirement is to know how to forgive.

When the pain we suffer stems from moral evil, caused by the free agency of another person, the first reaction is to become angry with the responsible party. This is normal; we would not be human otherwise.

But we must learn to have a second reaction: forgiveness. The choice is clear: Either we forgive, or we are overcome with bitterness. If we do not forgive, we end up channeling our pain in the worst possible way; we are filled with resentment, hate, and a desire for revenge. This is the worst way to process pain. A reaction of this nature is one of the principal causes of any war. And this not only applies to international conflicts, but also to family conflicts. When we retaliate against moral harm, divisions and hate grow among families and friends.

Forgiveness does not mean that we do not defend ourselves. If we have been the victim of injustice, it is within our rights to protect ourselves, even through the judiciary system if necessary. But it is one thing to defend ourselves and another very different thing to seek revenge. We should defend ourselves without hate or resentment, making an effort to find solutions and compromises without falling into the urge to destroy our opponent. Forgiveness means not harboring resentment or hate, not wishing harm on anyone.

Forgiving does not mean that we have not been hurt, for a wound always hurts. If someone we love wounds us physically by mistake, it would be easy to forgive, since we would quickly realize the person meant no harm, but the wound would still remain and bother us until it completely heals.

When someone treats us unfairly, even if we genuinely forgive, we may remember that injustice each time we see the wrongdoer. Although we do not wish the person any harm, it may be unpleasant to see or talk with that individual. This is normal; the wound needs time to heal, and the more serious the wound, the longer the healing may take. The important thing is that we do not hold resentment nor seek revenge, but that we aim to treat the person with kindness.

In his Letter to the Romans, St. Paul outlines a strategy for how to respond to moral evil:

> Repay no one evil for evil, but take thought for what is noble in the sight of all. If possible, so far as it depends upon you, live peaceably with all. Beloved, never avenge yourselves, but leave it to the wrath of God. . . . Do not be overcome by evil, but overcome evil with good. (Rom 12:17–21)

This passage perfectly addresses how to fight against evil and pain: Do not avenge yourselves; overcome evil with good. If we respond to evil with more evil, we start on a downward spiral whose ending we cannot predict.

Evil is not overcome with hate and resentment, but by knowing how to forgive and generously handing out good. When John Paul II visited Spain in 1982, he had an unforgettable encounter with young people in the Santiago Bernabéu Stadium in Madrid. His speech centered precisely on these words from St.

Paul, relating them with the Beatitudes. He said that Christ's words

> indicate a program to overcome evil with good. . . .
>
> When you know how to be worthily simple in a world that pays any price for power; when you are pure of heart among those who judge only in terms of sex, appearance or hypocrisy; when you build peace, in a world of violence and war; when you fight for justice in the face of the exploitation of man by man or of one nation by another; when with generous mercy you do not seek revenge, but come to love the enemy; when in the midst of pain and difficulties, you do not lose hope and perseverance in goodness, strong in the consolation and example of Christ and in love for brother man. Then you become effective and radical transformers of the world and builders of the new civilization of love, truth and justice, which Christ brings as a message.[5]

The best possible response to the problem of evil and pain is found in the entirety of Christian doctrine. Christian faith leads us, as we see in the words of St. John Paul II, to fight evil by choking it out with good.

But for this to succeed, it is necessary to confront pain, to be willing to offer a remedy, to give it a

5. John Paul II, *The Liturgy of the Word with Young People*, November 3, 1982, https://www.ewtn.com/catholicism/library/liturgy-of-the-word-with-young-people-3-november-1982-26078.

constructive and positive reason. In this same address, the Pope said,

> In this way, the man—and especially the young person—who approaches reading the word of Christ with the question: "Why does evil exist in the world," when he accepts the truth of the beatitudes, ends up asking himself another question: "What can we do to overcome evil with good?"[6]

Do Not Overemphasize Evil: There Is Always Much Good

Once committed to the fight against evil and against pain, we should maintain a proper perspective and not give evil more importance than it deserves. Every day we come across things, some more significant than others, that hurt us. This is the daily cross that Jesus spoke about.

We cannot ignore the great number of good gifts that God gives us every day. I have seen many people upset because of problems, some more serious than others, and I always remind them, "Give thanks to God for as many good things as you can." This is key. We have many more reasons to be grateful to God than we have problems to complain about.

If we make our life into a continuous complaint, we end up bitter and spread bitterness into the lives of

6. John Paul II, *Liturgy of the Word.*

the people around us. In contrast, if we handle problems with composure and a good attitude, as far as is possible, we lighten the burden of our suffering and the suffering of others.

Speaking in general, we humans have a certain tendency to turn ourselves into victims. When we are suffering for some reason, it is reasonable to seek out sympathy and understanding from others; this is good for us. But if we exaggerate the situation, we harm ourselves and exasperate the people closest to us.

We should meet the tribulations of this life with composure and a good attitude, not by exaggerating our suffering, which can easily become a habit. Things that make us uncomfortable and cause us pain are inevitable in this life. St. Josemaría wrote:

> Life is a matter of facing up to difficulties and of experiencing in our hearts both joy and sorrow. It is in this forge that man can acquire fortitude, patience, magnanimity, and composure.[7]

We should not invent problems or let our pain get blown out of proportion. There will always be one thing or another that bothers us. Life consists of "experiencing in our hearts both joy and sorrow," in the words of St. Josemaría. We must not be blind to the many beautiful and wonderful things in our lives.

---

7. Josemaría Escrivá, *Friends of God* (Scepter, 1981), no. 77.

Let us always remember that God wants us to be happy, and to bring happiness to others. If we overvalue pain, we cause others to suffer. On the contrary, if we soften the suffering, we contribute to the happiness of others, and we ourselves will be more content.

VIII.

The Reason for Pain

Reason and Purpose

So far, we have made reference several times to the reason for pain. Before we address this topic conclusively, let's clarify this a bit more.

The term *reason* is normally synonymous with *explanation*. Many times, we humans demand an explanation, demand to know the "why" behind what has happened. This question is normally answered with the cause behind the incident, with two main types of causes: the agent that initiated the action, or the final use, or purpose.

For example, a fire on a mountain can be explained by identifying how it started: lightning, a campfire that was not put out, or some other reason. However, most human actions are explained by their purpose: A highway is built to connect us, a house is to live in, a telephone is to communicate, a fire is for a cook-out.

We must point out here that to speak of purpose is to speak of the intentions of intelligent beings. In nonrational nature, we cannot define purpose so easily, but rather usefulness, which is always fixed and constant.

Inanimate objects (stones, mountains, rivers) almost never display any purpose. They may be explained by their cause, but they have no definite final purpose. At most, they have some usefulness. For example, rivers are useful to direct rainwater, or volcanoes are useful to alleviate pressure in the magma chambers. Still, we cannot ask what purpose the mountains or minerals have; we can only explain their origin.

In non-intelligent living beings, there are hints, but not completely clear purposes. It would make more sense to speak of their usefulness as well. Bird wings are used to fly and tree leaves are used in photosynthesis, to name two. It is true that both in scientific and colloquial language, we commonly speak of the purpose of living things, animals and plants alike, but this is analogical; it refers to an overly simplified purpose, a purpose that is always constant. For this reason, it would be better to speak of usefulness, which is determined by the nature of the thing itself.

Nevertheless, humans have the capacity to give things a purpose; we give things a function. This function is not intrinsic to their nature but is imposed by us. It is our will that creates the purpose, giving a new function to an existing object. At times, the purpose we give corresponds to the natural usefulness of the object. But in many cases, the same object can serve two opposite purposes: A rock can be used to build a house, to break a window, or to kill an animal with a slingshot. They are very different purposes, not inherent to the rock. They are purposes people have invented.

Furthermore, humans often change the original purpose (or the use) of things in the interest of our own needs. We turn bird feathers into decorations, animal skins into coats, a strong current into energy to run a mill. We can give purpose not only to concrete objects, but also to our actions. Two people may do the same thing but have completely different purposes. The classic example from the Gospels is of the Pharisee who prayed in the temple in order to exalt himself while a tax collector humbly prayed to ask God's mercy.[1]

This capacity to give purpose to things is a characteristic unique to humans that differentiates us from animals. For an animal, a stick is a stick. For a human, the stick has a purpose; it is used for something. It can help to start a fire, serve as a weapon, or contribute to the building of a cabin. Seeking purpose is a characteristic that is evident from the earliest stages of life. For example, a young child sees a shell or a stone and turns it into something else, giving it a purpose and building an entire imaginary world around it.

This point is important in helping us make sense of the reason for pain: Natural things do not have a reason on their own, other than the inherent characteristics of their nature. Most of the time, when we ask

1. See Luke 18:9–14.

about the reason for something, we are asking about its purpose. This, strictly speaking, is exclusive to intelligent beings. Humans, with their intelligence, discover different possible purposes and, with their free will, decide which of those purposes to employ.

In figurative poetical language, we could say that the purpose is already incorporated into the object. The great Michelangelo, when looking at a block of marble, said that the sculpture was already inside the block and he only brought it to light. But this is not true; inside the block there was only rock. The sculpture really existed in the mind and will of Michelangelo.

This is not subjectivism, but recognition of the facts. The purpose of an inanimate object is associated with the initiative and will of humans, and of God.

God is the one who gives purpose to all of creation. The entire universe has come from his hand and has an eschatological purpose that God gave it and that will come to fruition at the end of time. But God gives us freedom in this area as well. He gives us the possibility, within our limitations, to give diverse purposes to the things at our disposal. That is to say that one of the results of freedom is to be able to give purpose or reason to our actions and to the objects we use, purpose and reason that we give, and that God respects as he respects our freedom.

Logically, God wants us to use our freedom well, to do good and not evil. But as we saw in chapter three, he respects our decisions, even when they go against his will. He will therefore respect our decision, even if it is contrary to his desire.

The Alarm Bell

Things found in nature, as we have seen, have a particular use as part of their essence. Does pain have some reason, some use in and of itself? The answer is yes; both physical and moral pain are the warning signals that something is not right.

When an organ in the body is not working properly, it hurts. This is an alarm that sounds so that we pay attention and treat the problem. This facet of pain is good. For instance, one of the principal complications for quadriplegics is the lack of feeling all over the body. The quadriplegic could be burning his or her foot and yet not feel anything. This poses numerous dangers that require very close medical attention, as pain is necessary for the conservation of life. It serves a very important function as our alarm system.

The same applies to moral pain. Even though there is no physical wound, when someone treats us badly, it hurts—sometimes more than a physical wound. Here, too, pain is an alarm telling us that something is wrong; in this case, the relationship with the person who has treated us badly is damaged. This is why it hurts much more when the person who treats us unfairly is someone close, a person we loved or trusted.

The Senselessness of Pain

Apart from this use—which is significant—pain makes no sense on its own. Other than serving as an alarm system, pain is not useful for anything. It has no other purpose.

How should we react when pain shows up? In the first place, we must strive to accept it as it comes, without getting lost in esoteric questions or trying to find a reason that is not there.

The question "Why me?" demands a reason for the pain, but pain does not carry an inherent reason other than to sound an alarm. If I have liver disease, the pain lets me know that something is not right. While there is a medical explanation, I still have no answer to why this illness fell on me. It doesn't make sense to ask. Trying to find the answer would send me down a spiral of suffering, despair, and possibly depression.

When pain arrives, we should first and foremost resist being carried away by emotions. "Why me?" is a question driven by emotions. Thinking rationally, we can discard it; but the emotions may continue to nag us to find a reason.

This is logical. When we suffer, all our emotions are disrupted. This disruption can lead us to view everything through a negative lens, to get angry, to be filled with bitterness and resentment. We may find ourselves unable to be calm and collected in our thinking.

When we are faced with pain, we must be especially careful to think calmly and not be controlled by emotions. We must discard the question "Why me?" along with with the notion that the pain has come from God, either as a punishment or as a gift.

Pain and suffering, by their very nature, have no use, no purpose. However, suffering can be made into the reason for multiple secondary effects, positive or negative.

Finding a Reason for the Pain: Not "Why?" but "For What?"

Pain is a natural phenomenon, like any other. It has an inherent reason, a fixed and constant use as a warning signal. It has no other intrinsic reason on its own.

Nevertheless, any experience of pain, like all concrete objects and all human actions, can be given a reason and a purpose. Humans have the ability to give purpose to something that goes beyond its intrinsic use. The natural use of a river is to carry rainwater down the mountain. But humans can give it other purposes: to water crops, to supply water to a city, to mark a border, or to turn electric generators.

We can easily verify that pain, in addition to its original use, produces other consequences. It can make us bitter, envious, or angry. In contrast, it can help us to better understand others who are suffering, fill us with compassion, and bring us closer to God.

This is a result of having added, many times without realizing, a deeper purpose or reason to the pain. But it is essential to remember that there is no implicit purpose in the pain. This is why the same type of suffering can lead one person to despair and another person to a deeper love for God and others.

One example that serves as a paradigm is the contrast of the two thieves who hung on crosses on either side of Jesus. What was the reason for those crosses? They had no reason. They were a senseless torment, a way for a judge and an executioner to inflict suffering on the condemned for crimes that had been committed. Crucifixion is one of the most extreme examples of senseless pain. Yet, nevertheless, one of the criminals was saved through his pain. The other, as far as we know, only let the pain spur him on to feelings of bitterness and hate.

The two crosses were identical. Yet one of the two men used his cross for a reason: to express compassion and repentance, which ultimately led to his salvation. The reason did not come from the cross but from the man. The other man used his cross for the opposite reason, to express not compassion but contempt and to inflict insult and pain.

What do we do when we experience pain and suffering? We must give it a constructive purpose, a useful reason. Often people experiencing serious pain ask for a reason for the pain. The answer, although it sounds shocking, is undeniable: "It's up to you to decide the reason for this pain."

We should, therefore, change the question. We should not ask "Why?" but "For what?"

To ask "Why?" is to look for a hidden reason that can never be found. Instead of "Why?," we should ask "For what?"; we should ask if this suffering will make us a better or a worse person, if it will help us to reach heaven.

In pious language, we can speak about "finding the reason for the pain," as if pain had a hidden reason that needs to be discovered. This literal interpretation is not exactly correct. It is like Michelangelo's answer for *David*. Only in a figurative sense can we say that the statue was already inside the marble block before the artist had begun to sculpt. Only in the figurative sense can we talk about the reason for pain (aside from its inherent use as an alarm). We do not need to discover the reason; we must *provide* the reason, and each experience of pain will have the reason that we impart.

It is unquestionable that, although God has not equipped pain with a reason *a priori*, his hope is for us to give it a good reason, just as he expects that we use all things on earth correctly—that we use atomic energy to cure sickness and not to kill, that we use iron for constructive tools and not for weapons, that we use cinema as healthy fun and not for lewd entertainment. God has made us free, but his desire is that we give everything a positive purpose, even pain.

From a Human Perspective

Faith aside, from a purely human perspective, pain allows us the opportunity to give it a positive reason. When we suffer, we can better understand the suffering of others. We can empathize with what others are experiencing if we have gone through a similarly hurtful situation. It can be especially hard for young people to understand life's toughest situations, and this is at least in part because they lack experience in many areas, including pain and suffering.

Pain makes us more cautious, makes us stronger, encourages us to take on life with more resolution and fortitude, forces us to become patient, and helps us to mature. Pain often helps us, from a strictly human perspective, to know how to appreciate things and notice the gifts in our lives. When going through a seriously painful situation, it becomes very clear that many of the things that worried us before were inconsequential. On our routine days, we tend to overvalue certain superficial aspects of life; but when we face deep pain, we see more clearly what is really important.

We can make the reason for our pain self-improvement, service to others as we refuse to let sadness drag us down, and an end to frivolousness. But if we deal with pain in the wrong way, we let it fill us with impatience, sadness and bitterness. We feel like victims, lose hope, and become depressed.

When we posed the problem of pain in the beginning of this book, we spoke of the "scandal of evil."

We said that a scandal is anything that can separate us from God. Now we see that it is not so much the pain and suffering that separate us from God, but rather the reason we give to the pain and suffering. If, like the unrepentant criminal, we channel our pain into anger and bitterness, the pain becomes a scandal; it separates us from God. In that case, we should admit that we were mostly to blame, because we made the pain into a reason to stray from God.

We can also give pain a positive reason. It all depends on us.

IX.

What Does God Expect from Us?

Joy and Happiness

This is first and foremost what God expects from us: that we be happy. This is why God created us: God is the God of joy.

The Lord also expects us to be holy, as St. Paul writes: "He chose us in him before the foundation of the world, that we should be holy and blameless before him. He destined us in love" (Eph 1:4–5). And Jesus, in all his authority, said, "You, therefore, must be perfect, as your heavenly Father is perfect" (Mt 5:48). St. Peter insists, "But as he who called you is holy, be holy yourselves in all your conduct; since it is written, 'You shall be holy, for I am holy'" (1 Pt 1:15–16).

We cannot go into greater detail here about what holiness is and how to reach it. But we should point out that holiness is intrinsically linked with joy and happiness. Do you want to be a saint? Bring happiness to the people around you!

St. Francis de Sales famously said, "A sad saint is a sorry saint." Joy is a prerequisite for sainthood. Holiness requires us to be happy and to share happiness with those closest to us or at least to try. A family that is holy, a family that is near to God, should be a family full of peace and happiness. A Christian home should be, as St. Josemaría would say, "full of the light and joy that were in the home of the holy family."[1]

What does God expect of us? That we be holy, that we know how to love, that we demonstrate our love overflowing with peace and happiness, that we be happy, and that we help others to be happy. As we saw in chapter one, Pope Francis said,

> It is no longer possible to claim that religion should be restricted to the private sphere and that it exists only to prepare souls for heaven. We know that God wants his children to be happy in this world too.[2]

This is what God wants of us, and he has given us freedom to be able to collaborate with him in the task of helping those around us to find happiness.

God is the God of joy, and his desire is that we be joyful. Does this mean we are to be joyful even in the midst of pain? Doesn't that seem like a completely ridiculous theory? In many cases, it all depends not so much on the pain, but rather on how we handle

---

1. Josemaría Escrivá, *Christ Is Passing By* (Scepter, 1982), no. 22.

2. Francis, *Evangelii gaudium*, no. 182.

it. St. Josemaría writes, "Suffering overwhelms you because you take it like a coward. Meet it bravely, with a Christian spirit: and you will esteem it like a treasure."[3] Many times our despair sharpens the pain. Pain, when met with peace and composure, with bravery, and with a transcendental vision of life, is much easier to carry than it would be if we were to become locked into our suffering.

Our ultimate happiness will come when we reach heaven, but here on earth we can be very happy all the same. One of the conditions is that we don't let pain (small or large) make us bitter, and that we do not run away in terror when faced with even the smallest amount of pain.

So, the first step is to confront pain with serenity. The world will not end because I have a toothache, or because my company is failing, or because someone has committed a crime against me. We will do well to confront pain with composure. If we are afraid of pain, any small annoyance will cause us to lose hope; any difficulty will be turned into a tragedy. On the contrary, if we accept beforehand that life will always have troubles and annoyances, we will know how to accept them with peace and maturity, and, as a result, we will be much happier people. We will be more able to enjoy many good things in life and we will take the unpleasant things with a sense of humor.

---

3. Josemaría Escrivá, *The Way*, no. 169, in *The Way*, *Furrow*, *The Forge* (Scepter, 2004).

A Great Gift from Christ

From a human standpoint, even without consideration for God, we can accept pain nobly. But realistically, this is difficult, and there are few people who are able to remain optimistic if they have no supernatural reference. The capacity to give suffering a positive meaning is one of the clearest and most important contributions of Christianity.

Before Christ, pain was always synonymous with disgrace. Stoic philosophy[4] attempted a somewhat more positive perspective, arguing that pain is not inherently evil. But this regrettably fell short in its consideration of pain as indifferent, endured only through reason and self-discipline. For the rest of the pagan world, the predominant philosophy was epicurean and hedonistic, which viewed pain as the ultimate disgrace. This is reflected in the current worldview. The further we get from God, the stronger the hedonistic tendencies and the greater the rejection of any type of pain or suffering.

With his whole life, but most clearly with his death on the cross, Jesus taught us that the cross, although it had no reason in and of itself, could be given meaning and converted into a triumphant throne. Jesus, on the cross, defeated sin, demons, and death. The cross of Christ became an instrument of redemption!

In this way, meaningless pain acquires, thanks to the voluntary obedience of Jesus, a supernatural value

---

4. Pre-Christian Stoic philosophy took root in the 3rd century BC through the early Roman Empire.

so large that it serves for the forgiveness of the sins of all of humanity. His suffering—irrational on its own, a product of hate and envy—receives a new purpose, a different purpose, that Jesus voluntarily gives it in his freedom.

But remember that for the unrepentant thief, the same exact cross had no purpose other than to fill him with resentment. It is not the cross that gives us heaven. It is Jesus, making that infamous cross into the reason for our redemption.

This is the great gift of Jesus, in relation to pain. He teaches us that we can give suffering a purpose that will convert it into an instrument with which to gain heaven. With his death, Christ has taught us that we can give pain value—no longer human value, but supernatural.

St. Josemaría writes:

> The great Christian revolution has been to convert pain into fruitful suffering and to turn a bad thing into something good. We have deprived the devil of this weapon; and with it we can conquer eternity.[5]

This has been the great gift of Jesus: teaching us to turn pain into a source of love, into fruitful suffering. Before Christ, suffering was fundamentally a weapon of the devil, a reality that quickly led to despair and resentment. After Christ, we can use this same reality as an offering to the Lord, as a reason to draw closer to him.

---

5. Escrivá, *Furrow*, no. 887.

A Key to the Door of Heaven

Returning to the title of this chapter: What does God expect from us when faced with pain? The answer is clear: that we learn to imitate his Son Jesus, that we learn to convert pain into a key to the door of heaven. How is this done?

In the first place, we must deal with pain well from a human perspective. We must not despair nor become obsessed with the question "Why me?" nor make ourselves into the victim. We should forgive when necessary, without sowing bitterness around us. We should be grateful for the concern of others for us, try to be happy and friendly, thank God for all the good things we have, and, additionally, peacefully employ the means available (medicine, for example) to alleviate our suffering as much as possible.

This simple list alone is in no way easy. We will need a calm and mature character to be able to bear pain well. But this is indispensable if we want to give pain a supernatural reason: We cannot expect our despair, resentment, or hate to be an offering to the Lord.

It can be difficult, but not impossible. Almost any human reality can be redirected to the supernatural realm. Jesus, on the cross, converted human suffering into an offering of love to God the Father. This sacrifice transformed the torment of the cross into a victorious throne.

And we can do the same ourselves. Christian mothers teach their children the value of a sacrificial offering at an early age. How pleasing to God are these little sacrifices offered in love! To be sure, this is also applicable to any human reality, not just to pain. We can offer the Lord our work, our joys, our free time, our meals, or our fasts. We can offer to the Lord any noble human action. And the more love we put into the offering, the more its supernatural value.

These offerings are especially valuable when made by a person experiencing illness. Many saints have written that the prayers of the children and the weak are especially pleasing to God. When a person who suffers (either by infirmity or by injustice) knows how to humanly bear the suffering well and to offer it to the Lord, this pain takes on a supernatural value that is difficult to match in any other circumstance.

We can give wonderful meaning to our pain. We can use it to make amends for our sins, or to intercede for others or for our own spiritual growth. Almost anything that we want to ask the Lord, if backed by the value of suffering, receives special attention. We must only learn how to bear our suffering with composure and patience and offer it with love to the Lord. Love transcends this world and converts pain into something incredibly valuable in the eyes of God.

Loving God's Will

A person of faith is accustomed to hearing people talk about love for the Cross, accepting the will of God, and seeing the will of God in every illness and pain. Many spiritual authors have reflected these ideas in their writing. For example, St. Francis de Sales writes:

> The Cross comes from God. We should not stare at it naively, but rather we should adapt to it, as we would with a person who has come to live at our side. One must not stop to think, but advance sweetly, accept with simplicity the things that come; not reflect on them too much, but take them as coming from the hand of God.[6]

We can also cite St. Josemaría:

> And if you ever have to bear unexpected blows, or undeserved tribulations at the hands of your fellow men, you will know how to sing with a new joy: "May the most just and most lovable will of God be done, be fulfilled, be praised and eternally exalted above all things."[7]

St. Thomas More, soon before he was martyred, consoled his daughter writing: "Nothing can come

---

6. Francis de Sales, *Epistolario*, 10.1. Our translation.

7. Escrivá, *Friends of God*, no. 167.

but that that God wills. And whatsoever that may be, no matter how evil it may seem to us, shall indeed be the best."[8]

A quick reading of these texts would lead us to believe that these trials are the will of God, as if God were sending us bad things. We need to be reminded that most of these texts should not be read in the literal sense. Take, for example, the historical case of St. Thomas More. He would soon be unjustly executed; he would die a martyr for defending the faith in obedience to the Pope. The phrase, "Nothing can come but that that God wills," should not be understood textually. His death was an injustice, a martyrdom, a great sin on the part of those who condemned him to die. God cannot want the murder of an innocent man, which is what happened. God cannot want a moral evil, which always entails sin. This is the doctrine of the Church: "God is in no way, directly or indirectly, the cause of moral evil."[9]

So then, why do these authors (who are saints!) say these things?

What is going on is similar to what happens with math teachers. If they are careless when explaining a long and complicated theorem, they skip a step during the demonstration. For them, the missing step is obvious, but for the students, it is not.

---

8. Thomas More, *The Correspondence of Sir Thomas More*, cited in the *Catechism of the Catholic Church*, no. 313.

9. *Catechism of the Catholic Church*, no. 311.

Allow me to explain in a bit more detail. God does not want anything bad to happen to us. As we have seen, evil comes through the free actions of humans or through the natural processes of nature. But it is the direct will of God that we confront hardships with peace and composure, that we do not despair or become resentful, that we forgive, that we give a positive reason to the pain, and that we return evil with good. This is the will of God, explicit and repeatedly revealed. God does not want evil. But he does want us to bear it well.

"If any man would come after me, let him deny himself and take up his cross daily and follow me" (Lk 9:23). These same words of Jesus are repeated almost identically in Matthew 16:24 and Mark 8:34. The three writers of the Synoptic Gospels took note of these words almost without variation, and in this way demonstrate their importance and the impact they had on the audience.

But please notice that Jesus did not say, "If any man would come after me, I will give him crosses." Jesus, God, does not give us any cross; he does not send us suffering or pain. The evil that can befall us is not the will of God. But it is the will of God, taken from these words, that we know how to carry the cross with grace as we follow Jesus.

Going a step further, it is the will of God that our small daily crosses serve to bring us closer to God, not to separate us from him. It is the will of God that we make our pain into a reason to draw closer to Jesus, not a reason to fall into resentment and despair.

Therefore, in the face of pain, we should love the will of God. But this will of God—that we should love—is not itself the cause of the pain, but rather his desire that we carry our suffering well. And if we do carry it well, any pain is automatically converted into a great supernatural good. Even martyrdom, motivated by love for God, should be the greatest supernatural good to which a person can aspire. This is why St. Thomas More believed that nothing bad could happen to him: From a heavenly perspective, even his unjust death due to his love for God was a great good.

In the quote above, St. Josemaría said, "If you ever have to bear . . . undeserved tribulations at the hands of your fellow men . . ." This means that when someone, in complete use of his or her freedom, in complete opposition to the will and commands of God, commits a sin or an injustice against us, we will, in the words of St. Josemaría, "know how to sing with a new joy: 'May the most just and most lovable will of God be done, be fulfilled, be praised and eternally exalted above all things.'"

What is this will of God? To be sure, it is not that we suffer injustice. There is no way that this can be the will of God, since God could never want sin. Sin was the will of the one who carried out the injustice. And yet, there is a will of God to be loved: that we bear the injustice well, that it be used to unite us with the Cross of Christ, that we return good for evil. This is the most just and most lovable will of God, which we should desire.

Having understood this, it becomes easier to make sense of the statements quoted above. How can we help a pious person see how to handle pain correctly? With a reminder that pain should be accepted as if it were the will of God. St. Francis de Sales affirms this: "Do not reflect on them too much, but take them as coming from the hand of God." He is not saying that the cross comes from God, but that we should take it *as if* it had come from the hand of God. This statement says a lot for a pious person; it speaks of resignation and serenity; of offering pain; of being united to the Cross of Christ; of forgiveness—all of which is enormously helpful in processing pain.

But we should never say something like this to someone who is not prepared to understand this most just and most lovable will of God, which expects us to give pain the positive reason we have been discussing. If a person does not live out a coherent and deep Christianity, it will be quite difficult for the person to understand a statement of this type.

To carry pain as God expects requires from us an act of will. "We should accept mortification with those same sentiments that Jesus Christ had in his Holy Passion."[10] Mortification, whatever suffering may cause it, is not sent by God; but Jesus leaves us the example of how to accept it, how we can turn it into the key that opens the door of heaven.

---

10. Josemaría Escrivá, *The Forge*, no. 406, in *The Way, Furrow, The Forge* (Scepter, 2004).

One last clarification to help us understand in what sense we can say that a sickness, for example, is the will of God: In chapter three, when we discussed the power of freedom, we explained that there is a difference between God's universal will and his particular will. The bad things that may happen to us all fall logically within the universal will of God, who has wanted this world to be just as it is, with human freedom and complexity in nature. And I will remind you that both freedom and complexity are great goods; that is why God wants them.

Therefore, we can affirm the universal will of God: that we live this life and know how to carry the pains and the joys of this world, that we be sanctified through ordinary daily events, good and bad alike. For this reason, when faced with any pain, it is correct to say that we should love the will of God, without losing sight of the fact that we are referring always to the universal will of God. But we can never affirm that any concrete evil is the particular, express will of God. It can never be said that a specific illness or any other trouble was what God wanted, as if he were guilty of inflicting the illness we are suffering.

God designed the world exactly as he wanted, with its struggles and pleasures, and additionally, he has provided the means necessary that we may be sanctified through both hardships and joys.

Co-Redeemed: United to Christ on the Cross

Therefore, a person of faith can make pain into something supernatural, using it to ask for forgiveness for sins or to pray for grace.

Furthermore, we can give the greatest possible meaning to any experience of suffering. It can become a reason to unite us to the Cross of Christ, to help bring about the redemption that Christ accomplished on the cross. When Jesus gave up his life on the cross, he redeemed the entire world with his obedience and with his pain. Nevertheless, this redemption must be freshly applied to each individual person.

This is the most excellent meaning we can give to our pain. In a letter addressing suffering, Pope John Paul II writes:

> In bringing about the Redemption through suffering, Christ *has* also *raised human suffering to the level of the Redemption.* Thus, each man, in his suffering, can also become a sharer in the redemptive suffering of Christ.[11]

For a person who is in love with God, this is sufficient to almost make us wish for pain. If pain can receive such a high supernatural value, we can find ourselves saying, "Blessed be pain!"

---

11. John Paul II, *Salvifici doloris,* no. 19.

But this can only be understood with a strong supernatural vision, only when we love God so much that we are willing to give our very life to love him more, and to help others love him as well.

When this inner desire is present, then we have the key to take on suffering with peace, no matter how great it may be. Pope Benedict XVI wrote:

> It is not by sidestepping or fleeing from suffering that we are healed, but rather by our capacity for accepting it, maturing through it and finding meaning through union with Christ, who suffered with infinite love.[12]

For this reason, the way we deal with our pain and the reason we give to our suffering are very clear indicators of our faith and our love for God.

With this in mind, we can more clearly understand the differences between direct and pious language. Pious language takes for granted that, in the face of pain, the reasons have already been conferred. From that point on, the pain, a consequence of some type of evil, ceases to be evil and is converted into a great supernatural good.

One of the clearest examples of this incongruity in language is found in the writing of St. Josemaría:

> I will tell you which are man's treasures on earth so that you will appreciate them: hunger, thirst, heat,

12. Benedict XVI, *Spe salvi*, no. 37.

> cold, pain, dishonor, poverty, loneliness, betrayal, slander, prison. . . .[13]

If we employ literal meaning, to affirm that hunger, thirst, and betrayal are good (a treasure) is a crazy proposition. Each of these things is, on its own, bad, a producer of pain and suffering.

If there is one thing important for an ordered life, it is not calling good what is bad, or bad what is good. And all of the items on that list are bad, not good. How is it possible that the author calls them "treasures?" It is because he is using pious language, and, furthermore, has skipped a step, has assumed that the reader experiencing these types of suffering has been able to give them supernatural meaning. In that case, all of these evils have reached their fullest and deepest possible meaning; they are converted into a tool to reach heaven and to help in the redemption of all human realities. For a person of faith, there is no greater treasure on earth.

God Is Near to Those Who Suffer

Is everything we've just described just a utopian dream? Isn't it nearly impossible to take on pain in this way?

Of course, it would be a full-on utopian dream if we were to rely only on our own strength. But we should keep in mind, especially in the most painful moments, that "God is always near to those who

---

13. Escrivá, *The Way*, no. 194.

suffer." This quote is practically a fixed expression in Christian circles, with good reason.

In the Gospels, Jesus gives us a long list of examples of how he cares for those who are burdened with pain: the lepers, the blind, and the paralyzed. Not one suffering person who approaches the Lord is despised by him. But not only this; without anyone even asking, Jesus cures the paralytic by the pool of the portico, resurrects the son of the widow of Nain, heals the man with the withered hand, revives Peter's mother-in-law, and casts out the demons of the man possessed in Gerasene. In many opportunities, without anyone saying anything, Jesus takes the initiative and goes to the suffering person to bring healing.

Above all, by dying on the cross, God has demonstrated that he is close to those who suffer. With his death, Jesus testified beyond any doubt that he shares our pain and our despair and, at the same time, set the example of how to respond to suffering.

This is another great gift of Jesus: He demonstrated, with his life and with his death, that he is near to us, that he has suffered with us and for us. The Spanish philosopher García Morente tells the story of his conversion after having tried fruitlessly to find God through philosophy:

> The distance between my poor humanity and the theoretical God of philosophy had become an impasse for me; too far, too foreign, too abstract, too geometrical and inhuman. But Christ, this God

> made man, Christ suffering like me, more than me, much more than me, him I could understand, and he understood me.[14]

We cannot think that God does not understand pain. He does; he has experienced it.

No one who is suffering should feel alone. When we must endure pain, God is closer than ever, gazing at us with more affection than we can even comprehend. The Lord is always at our side, giving us his grace and strength, especially in moments of pain. This certainty is of great help when the time comes to endure pain with serenity and patience, when it is our turn to give pain a positive meaning, humanly and supernaturally.

In this regard, it seems important to remember one additional point. God regularly intervenes in human history through persons who freely dedicate their lives to doing the will of God. God helps those who suffer, not only with his grace but also through the involvement of others nearby who demonstrate compassion, who care for and help the afflicted, who will not leave a neighbor to bear suffering alone.

That is to say, God expects us to be agents of mercy, to help whoever may need it. Anyone who must endure pain should be able to recognize the love of God in us. This is the lesson taught in the Parable of the Good Samaritan (see Lk 10:30–37). God makes

---

14. Manuel Garcia Morente, "*El hecho extraordinario.*" Our translation.

himself present through others to those who are experiencing pain. He wants to use us as instruments of his compassion.

As Christians, we should all keep this in mind and act on it. Health professionals and other caregivers, in particular, should keep this at the forefront of their thinking. Doctors, nurses, and those who care for the elderly are the hand of God in the fight against pain and illness. They will do well to ask the Lord to help them see the suffering face of Jesus in every patient.

Smile in the Midst of Pain

What does God expect of us when we face pain? He desires that we give it a positive meaning, that we be united to the Cross of Christ, that we make our pain an offering, and *even* that we learn how to smile in the midst of the pain. Isn't this going a little too far? No, it is possible; we have seen this in the lives of many saints. Without searching further, we have the example of John Paul II, on the verge of death, smiling and being kind to all around him. In the days before his death, he continued to appear in the small window of the Vatican, waving affectionately to those who had come to see him.

Any difficulty can cause pain. But pain, if we do not properly deal with it, will in turn produce a different kind of evil that can be worse than the initial evil. We might find ourselves stuck in a pit of suffering, a pit of selfishness and self-pity. This is another evil, more dangerous than the first, and a reason for sadness, despair, and depression. To smile in the face of pain, even if it seems forced, helps us to remember that we are not alone, and that we should continue to demonstrate love and concern for the people we have at our side, even in the midst of our pain.

Understandably, a person on the verge of death does not normally have the strength to smile at anyone. But most types of pain are not so serious. We can overcome evil with good. We can overcome pain with a smile and a positive attitude.

There is a famous saying from St. Paul that sums up a great truth: "We know that in everything God works for good with those who love him, who are called according to his purpose" (Rom 8:28). Or, in the familiar and concise Latin, *omnia in bonum*, "everything is for good." These three words sum up everything we have explained in these last chapters. When we respond well, when we can find the positive reason, even pain can bring much good. It can make us more patient, more thoughtful, more compassionate; and it can help us to understand others. Above all, it can lead us to be more closely united to Christ and draw us toward heaven.

In this way, we will feel within ourselves the joy of participating with Jesus in redemption, and this will make us so happy that it will be evident in our smile.

The God of Joy

We are coming to a close. I hope this book has helped you to see God with a different perspective. God is the source of all good, all love, all joy. He is in no way a god of death or of punishment. He is not the cause of sickness, pain, or evil in the world. God is, on the contrary, always by our side, teaching us and helping us to bear our suffering. He even gives us the example of how to turn pain into joy, into an instrument of love.

With his life, Jesus teaches us that the road to happiness is not one of comfort and pleasure. Neither do we find happiness in the absence of worries and pain, as some Eastern philosophers propose. The road to happiness, and to holiness, is always the road of love.

The great challenge posed by pain is to convert suffering into an opportunity to love. When we see suffering people, we must kindly and tenderly come alongside them, helping them to carry their burdens and not feel alone. When it is our turn to bear a burden, we must give meaning to the meaningless pain, make it into a reason to love God and others.

When St. John of the Cross managed to escape unjust and painful imprisonment in 1578, he arrived at the convent of Carmelitas Descalzas of Beas. Upon seeing him so badly wounded, the prioress sent two nuns to console him by singing songs. One of these songs was so moving that he begged them to stop singing. Then, meditating on the words, he quickly recovered. The song said:

> He who has not known sorrow
> in this valley of pains,
> has not known good things,
> has not tasted love,
> for sorrows are the garments of those who love.[15]

Evil and pain are not sent by God. The Lord gives good things, life, liberty, and joy. But we can succeed in turning pain into an instrument of love, into another opportunity for joy and happiness. And this is another great gift from God, the God of joy.

---

15. Ana de Jesús, "Liras en loor de los trabajos" in *Las primeras poetisas en lengua castellana* (Ediciones Siruela, 2016). Our translation.

Annotated Bibliography

First, the Gospels. The four Gospels, and the whole New Testament, are the primary source where we learn that God, Jesus, is the God of joy, of love and compassion toward those who suffer. This is the best place to learn about how to radically fight the evil that we encounter in ourselves.

Aquinas, Thomas. *Quaestio Disputata De Malo*, and some points of *Summa Theologica.* (1.22 on Providence, 1.25 on the omnipotence of God, 1.48–49 on evil, 1.103 on the government of the world). In other articles of *Summa Theologica*, there are references to the problem of evil and of pain in the world. For a philosophical study on evil and pain, St. Thomas Aquinas cannot be overlooked.

Cardona, Carlos. *Metafísica del bien y del mal.* Pamplona: EUNSA, 1987. This is probably the most complete book, in terms of philosophy, on the question. It follows Aristotelian-Thomistic metaphysics, with a good systemization of the problem of evil. A background in philosophy is needed to be able to enjoy this book.

Escrivá, Josemaría. *The Way*, *Furrow*, *The Forge*. Scepter, 2004. There are several points of meditation on pain and suffering in these three books, especially the chapter "Suffering" in *Furrow.*

Fabro, Cornelio. *El Pecado en la Filosofía Moderna*. Madrid: Rialp, 1963. A short philosophical book analyzing the failures of some existentialist and Freudian philosophies when it comes to confronting the problems of freedom, evil and conscience.

Francis, Apostolic Exhortation *Evangelii gaudium* (especially nos. 4 and 5). November 24, 2013. In general, this exhortation is based on the conviction that the doctrine of Christ is the best way to joy and happiness, and how we should make an effort to share this message with all people.

Francis, Encyclical Letter on Care for Our Common Home *Laudato si'*. May 25, 2015. This is a long letter from the Pope on the topic of caring for the world as the common home of all people, in which he exhorts readers to fight against evils that harm nature in all aspects.

Frankl, Viktor. *Man's Search for Meaning*. Originally published in German as *Ein Psycholog erlebt das Konzentrationslager* in 1946. The author was a famous psychiatrist from the School of Vienna (the school of Sigmund Freud). Of Jewish descent, he was a survivor of Auschwitz. In this book, he describes his experience in the Nazi concentration camps and how there, in the middle of unimaginable horror, he found meaning in life by helping others and forgetting about himself. It is required reading for anyone who wants to go deeper on the subjects of pain and evil.

John Paul II, Apostolic Letter on the Christian Meaning of Human Suffering *Salvifici doloris*. February 11, 1984. This is a long letter that the Pope wrote for the Year of Redemption, focused on the meaning of suffering.

John Paul II, *Homily for the Youth Gathering in Santiago Bernabeu Stadium*, Madrid, November 3, 1982. See also his speech for the *World Youth Day Prayer Vigil*, 2000. These reflections are not about pain specifically, but they do address evil in society and the need to overcome evil with good. They are short texts and written for youth, with simple and accessible language.

Lewis, C. S. *A Grief Observed*. London: Faber and Faber, 1961. Lewis wrote this book upon the death of Helen Joy Davidson Gresham, his wife who died of cancer. The book was made into the movie *Shadowlands*. Comparing this book with *The Problem of Pain*, we find a great difference in addressing the problem of pain from a theoretical viewpoint, and how we feel when affected personally. All the same, a warning is necessary: This book, a literary gem, in my opinion does not resolve the problem of suffering in first person. Lewis's reaction, described by himself, does not seem completely correct.

Lewis, C. S. *Mere Christianity*. New York: Macmillan Company, 1952. A good book that compiles radio talks that Lewis gave between 1942 and 1944 on diverse topics related to the faith. One of the chapters, "The Perfect Penitent," is interesting for the study of repentance.

Lewis, C. S. *The Problem of Pain*. London: The Centenary Press, 1940. This book was written by a great thinker. It is a worthwhile read. He takes a correct approach to the problem with a somewhat polemic tone, as with almost all his writing. It is fundamentally theoretical; he does not address how to handle pain personally.

Maritain, Jacques. *Saint Thomas and the Problem of Evil*. Lecture given at a conference in 1944 at Marquette University in Milwaukee, and published that same year as chapter seven of the book *From Bergson to Saint Thomas*. This is a short philosophical talk in which he presents and explains St. Thomas's line of thinking about evil. The conference can be found on the internet.

Monge, Miguel Ángel. *Luz sobre el sufrimiento y la muerte*. EUNSA, 2012. The author attended numerous ill patients and writes this book from the perspective of helping them to understand and process the suffering of sickness.

Morales, José. *El Misterio de la creación*. EUNSA, 1994. Chapter fifteen, "La cuestión del mal," is dedicated to this topic within the theology of creation.

Nathanson, Bernard. *The Hand of God*. Washington, DC: Regnery, 1997. This is not a theoretical book about the problem of evil, but a personal testimony from the so-called "abortion king" and his conversion process when he began to realize the evil of abortion.

Vilar y Planas de Farnés, Johannes. *Antropología del dolor*. EUNSA, 1998. The author attempts to understand the phenomenon of pain from an anthropological (human) point of view.